Tales from the LSU Sidelines

A Captivating Collection of Tiger Football Stories

By Lee Feinswog

Sports Publishing L.L.C.
www.sportspublishingllc.com

©2002 Lee Feinswog
All rights reserved.

Director of production: Susan M. Moyer
Project manager: Jim Henehan
Dust jacket design: Kerri Baker
Developmental editor: Erin Linden-Levy
Copy editors: Cindy McNew & Ashley Burum

ISBN: 1-58261-346-x

Printed in the United States of America

Sports Publishing L.L.C.
www.sportspublishingllc.com

Contents

Introduction

When Sports Publishing presented the idea that I write a book about LSU football, a number of different paths popped up. There have already been histories and biographies and collections about LSU football, so the thought was to go in a different direction and find some stories and angles that you might not have heard of or read about before. In other words, I decided another rehash of the 1958 national-championship season and recounting Billy Cannon's punt return, well, that wasn't for me.

So I stayed away, more or less, from the obvious and tried to come up with some anecdotes and tales that the LSU football fan might find out of the ordinary.

Few things, of course, are more out of the ordinary than LSU football. Few places besides Louisiana attract such a rabid following in which the game becomes an event unparalleled in the community.

I've likened it over the years to Baton Rouge's version of the opera, where anyone who's anyone gathers with more than 90,000 of their closest friends seven times a year.

To call LSU football a happening is an understatement. It's ingrained and woven into the sporting culture in Louisiana in a way that sometimes boggles the mind.

Jarvis Green, who was a senior in 2001, is a product of Donaldsonville, Louisiana, just half an hour downstream from campus in the shadow of the Sunshine Bridge over the Mississippi River. Though plenty of players have come to LSU from out of state and been stars, for kids from Louisiana who come to LSU, there's simply something special about being a Tiger.

Green's career, capped with LSU's Sugar Bowl victory over Illinois, was no different.

"I cried for about 30 minutes after the game," Green admitted.

Jim Collier, an LSU assistant coach from 1965-79, was a recruiter who admitted he didn't always have to work that hard. "We had players there who would have come there without a scholarship," Collier said. "It was tradition."

Joe Dean, LSU's athletic director from 1987-2001, easily summarized the key to being a good AD: "Have a winning football team."

The people involved with LSU football who were interviewed for this book genuinely enjoyed talking about it, from the players to the coaches to the administrators. I wish I could have talked to everyone who wore the purple and gold. Instead, I simply had freefalling conversations with the ones I did contact, generating the interesting stories that appear in the pages ahead.

Herb Vincent was LSU's sports information director for 12 years, leaving for another career in 2000. Vincent, whose job made him live, breathe and sleep LSU football, probably best summed up what LSU football means.

"It's so big there," Vincent said. "It's so big in Baton Rouge, which is a good thing. Some people become a little too obsessed with it. But on the other hand, it's always a release for people. It's always something that's good for Baton Rouge and Louisiana.

"Even when they're losing, it is something good. It's something besides the politics and the school system. You know, all those things you always hear about Louisiana, how they're last in this and last in that and last in this.

"What's amazing to me, too, is the tradition that goes with it. The family traditions. How many people grew up always going every Saturday. It's what they do."

Vincent paused and smiled.

"It amazes me that there are so many people who don't have a whole lot of money, yet who budget their whole year making sure they have enough for LSU football. They're always going to a bowl game if LSU is going to a bowl game.

"Some people always budget for their summer vacations. Well, these people budget for LSU football and everything that goes with it. And that's what's amazing to me."

Amazing it is.

Lee Feinswog
May 2002

CHAPTER 1

Opening Hits

When you think of LSU football, you might visualize the roar of the fans, 92,000 strong in Tiger Stadium, or Mike the Tiger taking his pregame lap around the field, capped with a deafening roar, or the goosebumps you might get when the Golden Band from Tigerland takes the field with all of its pomp and circumstance half an hour before kickoff; or you might reflect on the aroma of tailgating, an incomparable eat-a-thon and drink-a-thon on a Saturday in Baton Rouge.

Eventually, you would think about those moments when you watched the LSU football team win a big one or lose a tough one. The players have the strangest recollections of all.

Shaved Heads and All

Tyler Lafauci is regarded not only as a former LSU great, but also as a fantastic individual who goes out of his way to help anyone he can. His company, Baton Rouge Physical Therapy-Lake, is on the forefront of helping area high school athletic programs.

The product of De La Salle High School in New Orleans, where he was an All-American, was a first-team offensive guard on the Associated Press All-American team in 1973.

Tyler Lafauci. Courtesy of LSU Sports Information.

He took the field for the first time as a Tiger in 1971 during the season opener against Colorado in Tiger Stadium.

"We thought Colorado was going to come in here and die because of the weather. But they had a great team," Lafauci recalled.

"We had good two-a-days. I remember it was long. That was my sophomore year, and I was moved to defensive tackle. We had an inexperienced defense, seven sophomores starting on defense, but our offense had Bert Jones and real good experience. So we knew we had to outscore people and hold on defensively."

"It was great, it was packed, 67,000 people, and it was everything people say it is. You're excited and you don't know what to expect. But when you go out, there's that significant, significant roar.

"You know, it means something because all those people are really excited about you playing, being part of the team, but you can get caught up in it, like, 'They really are coming to see me play.' And it makes you have an even greater desire to achieve your potential. It was great."

Colorado, of course, was expected to wilt in the Baton Rouge heat and humidity.

"I remember in the first timeout," Lafauci said. "They took their helmets off and they were all shaved. This was in 1971 and they were all bald, and that shocked us," Lafauci said with a laugh.

"I played against a guy with a tattoo, but I'd never seen that before. It was a competitive game, but we lost [31-21] and it was kind of disheartening, playing and losing. But it was a great experience."

Ouch, That Had to Hurt

Quarterback Tommy Hodson (LSU 1986-89), will never forget playing at Kentucky in the fifth game of his freshman season.

"I hadn't yet solidified myself as a starter. I really needed to do something to fortify my starting role," the product of Matthews, La. recalled.

"Anyway, I threw an outcut to the left and they were blitzing. But they blitzed about every down back then. They

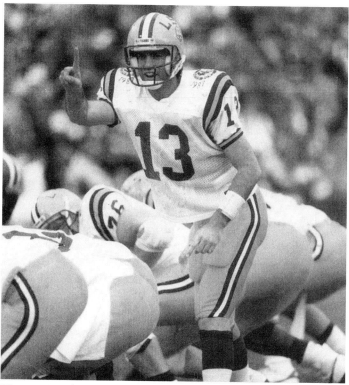

Tommy Hodson. Courtesy of LSU Sports Information.

were a real physical football team. They weren't very good, but they were really physical and played hard.

"I don't remember who it was, it was one of the outside linebackers, and when I turned to my left to throw, I just opened my body up, he hit me beneath the chin, and I bit through my tongue."

Dr. Sonny Carona, a Baton Rouge dentist who was with the team, took Hodson into the dressing room. "He stuck a probe through my tongue. I was kind of out of it, kind of incoherent. He stuck that probe through there and said, 'Well, you bit all the way through it.' He numbed it and put some deadening stuff in there. And he put three stitches on top and two on the bottom and closed it up."

LSU trailed 7-0.

"Coach Arnsparger said, 'Get back in the game.' I thought I was going to sit out the rest of the game. He said to get back in and I said 'OK.' I just went in there and started throwing the ball around and didn't care about much. I don't think my mind was right."

LSU rallied behind Hodson, who threw a couple of touchdown passes and completed 16 of 24 passes for 255 yards with no interceptions en route to a 25-16 victory.

"Wendell Davis had a big game and Brian Kinchen caught a big touchdown pass. So it was a big game. And people just thought it was the biggest thing, that I bit my tongue and played."

Of course, it wasn't like he just bit his tongue. He bit through his tongue.

"The story grows. The legend grows."

Luckily, Hodson wore a mouthguard, so no teeth were hurt and his jaw was OK.

"The only thing I have is a little scar beneath my chin," said Hodson, whose tongue completely healed.

"Yeah, I never had any problems, but," he joked, "I took English as a foreign language. Speech never was my big thing, but I don't think I had the tongue to blame for that."

A Great Turnaround

Trev Faulk left LSU after his junior season, choosing to enter the 2002 NFL draft. But the star linebacker from Lafayette, La., wasn't chosen. Though probably not surprising, Faulk's attempt to turn pro certainly did not indicate how well Tiger fans expected him to fare at the next level.

His last year at LSU turned into something special, but it didn't appear it was going to be that way after the Tigers fell to 4-3 overall and 2-3 in the SEC, with a 35-24 home defeat to Ole Miss.

"A lot of people got down on us, saying it was the same old thing," said Faulk, who was a starting freshman during LSU's 3-8, 1999 season, the Tigers' eighth losing season in 11 years. LSU did rebound with an 8-4 mark in 2000 under first-year coach Nick Saban, but attitudes remained unchanged.

"Even our coaches got down on us. The fans are fans; they're real passionate. But it made us really get close, especially on the defense," Faulk said. "We knew that we had to take care of each other, and it was like us against the world."

The "us" won, as LSU remarkably reeled off six victories to end the season, including a decisive win over Tennessee in the SEC championship game and another over Illinois in the Sugar Bowl.

Trev Faulk. Courtesy of LSU Sports Information.

The Big Switch

In 1965, LSU beat Arkansas in the Cotton Bowl. One of the stars on that team was Doug Moreau, an All-American split end who also handled LSU's place-kicking chores. Most of the time, that is.

He and LSU quarterback Billy Ezell had other plans, especially late in LSU's regular season-ending game against Tulane.

Understand that in 1958, the year LSU won the national championship, the Tigers ended the regular season with a 62-0 victory over Tulane. The exact same outcome occurred in 1961, and there was speculation about a third such blowout in 1965.

Moreau explains what happened late in the 1965 game: "This was a long-time-in-coming plan, because Billy was the holder for the three years that I kicked. We'd always

Doug Moreau. Courtesy of LSU Sports Information.

planned that when we had the opportunity, he would get to try a kick.

"So the last game of our senior season was against Tulane, and it was in Tiger Stadium. As the game went on, we're up there in the 30s, there was no question that we could score whenever we wanted. So the way the numbers were working out, we had 48 and figured out what we had to do [to win 62-0]. We had to score twice, and we wanted to exactly match the 62. And Tulane wasn't happy, because we were scoring pretty easily.

"So we're at 48 and we score, [but] we don't know if we're going to have enough time to score again, so this was the time, because Billy was waiting three years to try the extra point."

Billy and Moreau realized that if they made the extra point, they would bring the score to 55, making the desired final score only seven points away.

"So we line up, I'm holding, Billy's kicking and there you go."

Moreau laughed.

"But he missed!"

And Moreau laughed again.

"That's not what we expected and that's not what he was supposed to do. [But] what then happened is we got the ball back and we scored again. But because he had missed the extra point the last time, we went for two. Leading 60 to nothing. That really pissed them off."

Coach Charlie McClendon didn't say anything. Moreau speculated:

"I think he kind of knew that we always had that plan and Billy had the right to try one."

So as it worked out, LSU did match that 62-0 score for the third time in eight years.

"How many times do you get to go for two leading 60-0? But everyone, even Tulane, understood why we were doing it," Moreau said. "And what made it worse for them was they committed pass interference the first time we tried it, and we got to try it again. So we ran it over again and scored."

A Weak Back? Not Any More

Jarvis Green, a talented defensive lineman from Donaldsonville, La., starred on LSU's 2001 SEC championship team that beat Illinois in the Sugar Bowl.

But Green, who was the 28th pick of the fourth round in the 2002 NFL draft by the New England Patriots, spent his first two seasons in Baton Rouge in agony with a bad back.

For a while, his was the most talked-about back in Baton Rouge, because it was evident from the start of his career that Green would be quite talented, but a bad back has ruined many a man.

"It's kind of like a miracle the way it happened with my back," said Green, who was hurt so bad his redshirt freshman year that he avoided his hometown because so many people would ask him about it or try to help him with the slightest physical chores.

"I'm not handicapped," he sheepishly told people. After all, the young man is 6'3", 260 pounds. "But I stopped going back home."

Even at LSU, however, every time he practiced or played the media would ask about it. The injury occurred in a minor car accident. Green's car was bumped, and as a result, he suffered two fractured vertebrae and two bulging discs.

Jarvis Green. Courtesy of LSU Sports Information.

"We were in Donaldsonville, and one of my friends was riding behind me. We were looking at some girls on the right, and I slowed down but he didn't. He bumped me and we didn't even stop, because it was nothing.

"It's funny, because a year and a half later, I was driving with my brother and I got in an accident in Baton Rouge. Somebody hit us. I was driving, we spun around five or six times, and went into a ditch. It was about six in the morning because we were going to work. When we figured out where we were at, I was sitting in his lap in the passenger's seat. And I walked away from that fine. To this day, nothing."

But that wasn't the case the first time.

"It was killing me. I couldn't tie my shoes. I had to lay in the bed to do everything, including putting my shoes on. I played the whole season with it. It was painful, but in the

Notre Dame game [late in the 1999 season], it only got worse.

"I rested it for about two weeks and even went to a chiropracter. LSU helped me, too, but I needed more help. That spring and summer I didn't do any Olympic lifts and it was still killing me. We got to two-a-days and Coach [Gerry] DiNardo said he was going to limit my practices, but I still practiced. The last two days I got rest here and there."

Before the last scrimmage of the preseason, Green was hurting, but he still played well in a limited role. And then something strange happened.

"The next morning I was pain-free. Kenderick Allen was my roommate. The night before, I prayed for about 30 minutes and went to sleep and got up around 7:30 and we didn't have to be up till nine. I was moving around and Kenderick looked over and said, 'What the hell are you doing?'

"I was doing this," Green says, moving his arms around. "I was jumping around, hitting the wall, and I told him I didn't feel a damn thing! I jumped on the bed, was moving around. I went and told Jack [Marucci, LSU's director of athletic training]. He stretched me and it felt great."

In the scrimmage, Green had four sacks.

"It was funny, because as the season went on, I was scared it might come up again. But it never did. But that really humbled me a lot. The last two years I was up and down, but I was pain-free, and I thank God for that."

CHAPTER 2

Legendary Goal-Line Stands

LSU football is known for its many traditions and its hustling, all-out defensive pursuit. Simply put, LSU history resounds with some of the most dramatic goal-line stands in all of college football lore.

Historically, the Tigers have never been the biggest defenders, nor has LSU consistently produced high NFL draft picks in copious quantities. But when the Tigers have been at their best, it is because of those unheralded hustlers who take the fight to the big names when the ball–and the game–sit near the goal line. Interestingly, the big heroes of those goal-line stands have often been players whose overall LSU careers made them anything but stars.

The most recent of LSU's goal-line stands, a key defensive stop in the early fourth quarter of the Tigers' 31-20 2001 SEC Championship Game victory over Tennessee, is a prime example.

The victory, which gave LSU its first football conference title in 15 years, was a classic case of the underdogs knocking off the superstars. The goal-line stand was no different.

Tennessee entered the game with a 10-1 record and a No. 2 national ranking, having come off a dramatic upset of Florida in Gainesville. A win over LSU would catapult Phil Fulmer's Vols into a national championship matchup with Miami in the Rose Bowl.

Moreover, Tennessee boasted a team packed with future NFL stars, including high picks in the 2002 NFL draft, like wide receiver Donte Stallworth and defensive linemen John Henderson, Albert Haynesworth and Will Overstreet. All-league players like wideout Kelley Washington, quarterback Casey Clausen, tailback Travis Stephens and offensive lineman Reggie Coleman also sported orange and white. Tennessee had dominated the All-SEC team list published prior to the game, and most of the "experts" predicted a convincing defeat over an LSU team that managed to sneak into the championship game with a 5-3 conference record thanks to favorable tiebreakers.

The "experts" didn't get the game they expected. Stephens, who led the conference in rushing with 1,426 yards in the regular season, found battling against an unheralded Tiger defensive line tough. Clausen had found Stallworth and Washington open on three deep pass plays that helped the Vols build a 17-7 lead in the second quarter, but Tennessee's good fortune evaporated in the face of a furious Tiger rally. Backup quarterback Matt Mauck and backup tailback Domanick Davis lead the team after starters Rohan Davey and LaBrandon Toefield went down to injuries.

Mauck had vaulted the Tigers to a 24-17 lead by the end of the third quarter, but LSU's momentum seemed to be fading as the fourth period began. Capitalizing on three completions from his own 28, Clausen received a pass-interference call on Tiger cornerback Damien James for a first-and-goal at the LSU four. It seemed apparent that the Tiger lead—and the momentum—was about to vanish in the game's crucial moments.

Worse, as James was flagged for pass interference, LSU cornerback Randall Gay limped off the field with a twisted ankle. Tiger head coach Nick Saban, fresh out of substitutes to cover the corner, turned to freshman Travis Daniels—an erstwhile redshirt who had not seen the field all season long. Daniels, a promising practice player with a bright future, was as green as the Georgia Dome turf. Smelling blood, the 50,000 Tennessee fans in attendance began making their first real noises of the second half.

On first down, Washington was open in the left corner of the end zone on a fade route, but Clausen threw the ball over his head. LSU had dodged a major bullet.

On second down, the Vol quarterback moved in for the kill. Targeting the rookie Daniels, who was matched up with Stallworth on the right side, Clausen threw a quick slant at the goal line. But to his surprise, the freshman was ready. Daniels broke up the pass, earning his first touchdown-saving play on just his second down of college football.

Clausen threw for Washington again on a fade, and again the pass was outside the 6'4" receiver's grasp. It was now fourth down and goal, with the ball resting at the LSU four.

Fulmer still had an opportunity to earn a game-tying touchdown. LSU had held the line three times already, but a fourth seemed unlikely. It almost seemed like a college football version of the Cuban missile crisis, with Saban and Fulmer playing the roles of John F. Kennedy and Nikita Khrushchev.

And like Khrushchev, the Tennessee coach blinked. He sent in kicker Alex Walls for a field-goal attempt and settled for a four-point deficit at 24-20. LSU soon extended the lead to 31-20, when Saban sent in a running play rather than the field-goal unit on fourth and goal for the game-clinching score.

After the game, Tennessee fans were incredulous that no attempt was made to run the ball during the goal-line series. After all, the Vols boasted Travis Stephens, the SEC's leading rusher, and a huge offensive line. But the percentages favored Fulmer. Stephens had rushed for just 37 yards on 14 carries during the game and had been stuffed repeatedly on key plays. Clausen, on the other hand, would finish with 334 passing yards on the game.

"We just wanted to concentrate on stopping him and making them one-dimensional on offense," said LSU linebacker Trev Faulk of Stephens and the Vol rushing attack. "We accomplished what we set out to do."

Fellow linebacker Bradie James agreed. "They knew they couldn't run the ball on us," he said. "We took that away. And on that goal-line stand, we did what we had to do."

They did indeed. And in holding Tennessee out of the end zone on that fateful championship night, the 2001 Tigers made their mark in LSU lore by denying heralded players their place in the end zone.

The championship stand was merely the latest in a string of dramatic goal-line performances in LSU history.

September 30, 2000
"The Overtime Stand"
LSU 38, Tennessee 31

The stand in the 2001 SEC title game wasn't the first time Fulmer found himself burned by Saban's defense. Nor was it the first time that his passing attack failed him.

The Tigers, coming off an embarrassing loss to Alabama-Birmingham the week before, had played an inspired game behind new starting quarterback Rohan Davey. The junior, playing after a rib injury to Josh Booty the previous week, hit on 23 of 35 passes for 318 yards and four touchdowns, including a dramatic connection to tight end Robert Royal that put the Tigers ahead in the first overtime possession.

But now it was Tennessee's turn. Quarterback A. J. Suggs, who ultimately finished the game 37 of 59 for 319 yards and three touchdowns, moved the Vols to a first down on the LSU 11-yard line after a completion to Cedric Wilson and a run by Travis Henry. From there, Suggs hit Wilson again for seven yards to the Tiger four-yard line, bringing up third down and three, just 12 feet from Tiger Stadium's north end zone and a tied score.

But Tiger sophomore defensive back Damien James foiled Suggs's bid for glory. James, who three weeks earlier had made a key interception to end Houston's upset bid in the same end zone, knocked away a pass to David Martin on third down and repeated the feat on a fourth down pass intended for Eric Parker.

The LSU student section, whose ranks bulged near the front rows in the northwest corner of the stadium, burst onto the field after James's deflection, tearing up chunks of turf and tearing down the goalposts. It was the first signature victory of the Saban era and the first real sign that LSU was back after two years of desperation.

September 16, 1995
"The Magic Is Back"
LSU 12, Auburn 6

Though it ended in disaster, the Gerry DiNardo era at LSU began with one of the most dramatic victories in school history. At 1-1 after a loss to Texas A&M and a win over Mississippi State, both on the road, DiNardo's Tigers opened their home schedule against Auburn, ranked No. 4 in the nation. A crowd of 80,559, the second-largest in Tiger Stadium history, watched the proceedings.

The game was nip and tuck, as neither team was able to generate consistent offense. In perhaps the best play from the LSU offense, quarterback Jamie Howard executed a textbook tackle after an interception (no less than six of Howard's INTs had been returned for scores the previous year). The Tiger defense generated a goal-line stand of sorts, and defensive end James Gillyard punished AU quarterback Patrick Nix for a safety.

Nevertheless, the emotional Tigers failed to close the door on Terry Bowden's visitors, and as the game's waning moments approached, Auburn drove the ball to the LSU 11-yard line with a scant four seconds left.

But fate smiled on DiNardo and LSU. Cornerback Troy Twillie, whose LSU career before and after that September evening would be one of bitter disappointment, out-jumped

Auburn wide receiver Tyrone Goodson for a Nix pass in the northeast corner of the end zone to seal the LSU win.

Twillie's heroics proved pivotal in LSU's season. The 1995 Tigers, fielding a roster full of eventual NFL players, rode a roller-coaster campaign to a 6-4-1 regular season record. Without that Auburn win, LSU would never have been able to claim a bowl victory over Michigan State, and DiNardo's program would never have been on the college football map.

September 21, 1991
"Ricardo Comes Through"
LSU 16, Vanderbilt 14

For a time, DiNardo practiced magic in Baton Rouge. But it didn't come to him until he took the LSU job. His first visit to the city brought him nothing but heartbreak.

DiNardo's first year in Nashville coincided with the ill-fated opening of the Curley Hallman era in Baton Rouge. Hallman, who finished his career as the losingest LSU coach in modern history, had already suffered season-opening losses to Georgia and Texas A&M by a combined total of 76-17. In perennial cellar-dweller Vanderbilt, it appeared Hallman faced his best chance for an SEC victory all season.

But DiNardo had the Commodores playing above the cellar that season. Vanderbilt finished the 1991 campaign at 5-6, a record good enough to earn him the SEC Coach of the Year honor.

The game was a stalemate for 58 minutes, but it appeared DiNardo and Vanderbilt would close out a win. The

Commodores drove the ball to the LSU two-yard line with a last-minute possession and sent tailback Corey Harris, a 1991 second-team all-SEC selection, to dive over the line.

But LSU linebacker Ricardo Washington, a sophomore who had been a tight end the year before, met Harris at the goal line, and the ball popped loose. Senior cornerback Wayne Williams, who, like Washington, was a highly rated recruit with less-than-stellar college results, picked up the ball and raced 60 yards before being dragged down by Vandy QB Jeff Brothers. LSU then ran out the remaining seconds, and Hallman secured his first win.

LSU won four more games that season under Hallman, finishing with a 5-6 record, the best mark he would achieve (he managed another 5-6 campaign in 1993). The loss eventually cost DiNardo a winning season and a possible bowl bid.

September 3, 1988
"Lights-Out Defense"
LSU 27, Texas A&M 0

The Tiger defense was credited as a "lights-out" unit after carrying out an improbable goal-line stand during a convincing win over a highly rated Aggie team. Few knew that that Tiger team would also turn the lights out on winning football at the Ole War Skule for six long, painful years.

The 1988 season opened with what promised to be a tremendous matchup between LSU, coming off a 10-1-1 season, and A&M, riding an eight-game winning streak and a 10-2 mark in 1987. The Aggies were ranked as high as third in one preseason poll and were the odds-on favorite in the Southwest Conference.

But after the opening kickoff, there was little doubt that this Tiger team was a superior outfit. LSU dominated from the start, wiping the floor with Jackie Sherrill's Aggies once again.

In the midst of the victory, LSU's defense survived a bank of stadium lights going out as Texas A&M drove to the two-yard line. From there, the Tigers held Darren Lewis and the Aggies out of the end zone. One bizarre play occurred in which Aggie QB Lance Pavlas's pass banked off the south end-zone crossbar to a waiting receiver and touched off a meaningless A&M touchdown celebration.

No, this isn't an Aggie joke.

November 22, 1986
"Irish Eyes Are Crying"
LSU 21, Notre Dame 19

For classic goal-line stands, the 1986 stop of a talented Notre Dame squad is as good as any. That SEC championship Tiger team survived on toughness and hustle against one of the nation's best teams and in the face of horrendous adversity.

LSU went into the game ranked eighth in the nation with a 7-2 record, losing only in upsets to Miami of Ohio and Ole Miss. At 4-5, the Lou Holtz-coached Irish had been a snake-bitten team, with all five losses coming to ranked teams, four of them by a combined 12 points.

On that night, the Irish seemed worthy of the preseason hype. Notre Dame played a terrific game and seized momentum in the third quarter when a Steve Lawrence interception return gave them a first and goal on the LSU five-yard line. But three plays netted only four yards, giving Holtz a crucial fourth and goal at the LSU one-yard line.

This fourth-down play models the quintessential Tiger underdog story. The Irish goal-line offensive formation consisted of future NFL players, tight ends Joel Williams and Andy Heck, tackle Tom Rehder, center Chuck Lanza, quarterback Steve Beurlein, running backs Mark Green and Braxston Banks, and Tim Brown, a wide receiver who played halfback in the Irish full-house set. But on that play, they gained no purchase in the Tiger Stadium south end zone.

Holtz called for the option. Beurlein pitched to Brown, the future Heisman Trophy winner, only to see him stopped short of the goal line by Tiger cornerback Norman Jefferson and safety Steve Rehage.

"When we stopped Notre Dame on that goal-line stand, [nose guard] Darrell Phillips ran up to me on the sideline and said 'I knew they weren't going to score,'" Tiger defensive coordinator Pete Jenkins said years later. "I said to myself, 'I am glad he was so sure.'"

November 8, 1986
"Heartbreak for Humphrey"
LSU 14, Alabama 10

Tiger fans often lament "The Streak" when the subject of Alabama comes up. From 1969 to 2001, the hated Crimson Tide frolicked in Tiger Stadium without a loss. But many of the "woe is us" persuasion fail to remember that at one point during the Alabama malaise, a class of LSU seniors turned the tables on the Tide. In 1986, that class capped off three wins in Alabama in five years with a dramatic 14-10 victory.

And, naturally, it was a key goal-line stand that made the difference.

Tide tailback Bobby Humphrey, a future NFL player and all-SEC choice who would go on to establish a then-school record with 1,471 yards in 1986, fell just shy of a victory over LSU. With the Tigers ahead 14-10 midway through the fourth quarter, Humphrey took a handoff from quarterback Mike Shula and raced toward the goal line around the right side. But Tiger linebacker Eric Hill caught Humphrey before he could break the plane, stripping the ball in the process. Cornerback Kevin Guidry pounced on the loose ball in the end zone, saving a touchdown and ultimately LSU's winning streak in the Heart of Dixie.

"I didn't know the ball was loose," said Guidry after the game. "Then I looked around and the ball was rolling by my leg. I thought, 'What's that doing there?'"

November 3, 1979
"Fourcade Foiled"
LSU 28, Ole Miss 24

Ole Miss quarterbacks have periodically been a thorn in LSU's side. One who never could beat the Tigers, though, was New Orleans native John Fourcade. Though he eventually managed to tie the Tigers in 1981, his senior season, the sophomore from Holy Cross High School in New Orleans only found heartbreak in a 28-24 squeaker with the purple and gold in Jackson.

Fourcade's evening started off well. He led the Rebels to a 17-0 lead and then a 24-14 advantage with only six minutes to go. But Tiger running back Hokie Gajan initiated a late rally for the visitors by hauling in a pass in the flat and rumbling 52 yards for a touchdown. Wideout Tracy Porter followed the TD with a 49-yard punt return with a short reverse for the go-ahead touchdown.

Fourcade had his last chance to salvage victory with a little more than two minutes left in the game. He drove the Rebels to the Tiger nine-yard line for a first down and goal. As precious seconds ran off the clock, he threw an incomplete pass on the first down, then scrambled to LSU's three-yard line.

It was now do-or-die time for the Tiger defense attempting to stay above .500 in Charlie McClendon's final season (LSU was 4-3 at the time). Fourcade lofted a pass in the back of the end zone, but Tiger cornerback Willie Teal out-fought a pair of Rebel receivers for the football and the victory, preserving a winning record both for the season (LSU would eventually finish 7-5 with a Tangerine Bowl win over Wake Forest) and for McClendon's all-time mark against the Rebels. He finished 9-8-1.

"When Willie went up," McClendon said of the interception, "he looked 10 feet tall."

December 2, 1972
"Preserving the Streak"
LSU 9, Tulane 3

LSU hadn't lost to Tulane in 24 straight games since 1948. Three of these wins were by the improbable score of 62-0, but on this day in New Orleans, the

Bennie Ellender-led Green Wave appeared to be tightening the gap.

Neither team scored a touchdown the entire game, as Tulane's defense stymied Bert Jones and the LSU offense throughout the day. But as the seconds ticked off the fourth-quarter clock, Green Wave quarterback Steve Foley directed a last-minute drive toward glory.

Foley had a last-gasp opportunity at the LSU five, with no time-outs and only six seconds left. This would be the final play of the game. The future NFL defensive back rolled right and found halfback Russell Huber in the flat. Huber turned upfield and ran into the waiting arms of Tiger defensive back Frank Racine, who dragged him down one yard shy of a Green Wave touchdown as the clock ticked off the final seconds.

The close shave against the Green Wave put the finishing touches on a 9-1-1 regular season for Charlie McClendon's Tigers, who eventually dropped a game to Tennessee in the Bluebonnet Bowl and finished 9-2-1. LSU's streak over the Greenies would last no longer, as Foley engineered a 14-0 upset of a 9-1 Tiger team the next year.

November 25, 1972
"One Man's Burden"
LSU 3, Florida 3

Charlie McClendon's 1972 Tigers were probably best known for the last-minute heroics of Bert Jones and Brad Davis in their 17-16 win over Ole Miss. But perhaps the most dramatic individual effort that prevented an LSU loss might be that of sophomore cornerback Mike

Williams, the first African-American player in school history.

Williams, who was named a second-team All-SEC selection in his first year of varsity football, bailed out the sloppy Tigers in the midst of a Gainesville rainstorm. LSU was mired in a 3-3 tie with Florida despite the Tigers' nine field goal attempts by kicker Juan Roca, who missed a school-record eight of them.

Florida was on the verge of breaking the stalemate as speedy tailback Nat Moore, later a wide receiver for the Miami Dolphins, broke loose on a long run. But Williams ran down Moore at the one-yard line, and one play later he pounced on a Florida fumble to kill the drive.

Williams became a three-time second-team All-SEC selection, earning All-American recognition from *The Sporting News* in 1974. He blazed the trail for some of the best players in LSU history by breaking the color barrier at the Ole War Skule.

November 20, 1971
"Triple-Timing"
LSU 28, Notre Dame 8

Sophomore quarterback Bert Jones's arrival offset disappointing early losses to Colorado, Ole Miss and Alabama and helped LSU finish off the season with a 9-3 record. To get to the nine-win promised land, however, the 6-3 Tigers would have to fend off No. 7 Notre Dame, an 8-1 club featuring a gaggle of future pros.

They did just that, as Jones and Andy Hamilton made a mockery of the highly touted Irish secondary, and the smallish Tiger defense conducted several key goal-line stands.

Down 7-0, Ara Parseghian's visitors found themselves in an advantageous situation near the south goal line. It was fourth down and three inches to go for a first down inside the LSU one-yard line. Parseghian's offensive line, Jim Humbert, Frank Pomaricio, Dan Novakov, John Kondrk and John Dampeer, outweighed the LSU front by more than 30 pounds per man. Additionally, his fullback, Andy Huff, tipped the scales at a gargantuan (for that era) 218 pounds. A power running play seemed the obvious route to a tied ball game.

But as on so many other occasions, an outmanned Tiger defense refused to be out-fought. Parseghian sent Huff on an off-tackle play to the right side, only to see two hundred and five-pound defensive end Skip Cormier beat Dampeer and make initial contact behind the line of scrimmage. 205-pound linebackers Lou Cashio and Lloyd Frye resisted the powerful Notre Dame fullback and drove him back.

LSU's defense wasn't finished. Later in the game, the Tigers held on two stands in the north end zone. In the first, as Notre Dame played a fourth down and short just inside the LSU 10-yard line, cornerback Norm Hodgins dropped Irish QB Cliff Brown for a three-yard loss. Frye made his second touchdown-saving play by breaking up a Brown pass at the goal line on a fourth down and goal at the LSU three-yard line.

Afterwards, McClendon described the game by saying, "Gentlemen, there has never been a bigger victory in Tiger Stadium," and All-American defensive back Tommy Casanova compared the spirit of the Tiger team to that of Olympians who represent their country.

November 21, 1970
"No Heisman For Theismann"
Notre Dame 3, LSU 0

Ask a Tiger fan of the late 1960s and early 1970s vintage to name three or four of his favorite games, and invariably one of them will be an LSU loss. Some games were simply that good; the 1970 LSU-Notre Dame contest in South Bend was one of those.

As a result, one of the greatest goal-line stands in LSU history was actually incomplete and ended in the agony of a missed opportunity for the visiting Tigers.

The 7-1 LSU team, ranked No. 7 in the nation, traveled to South Bend to face an 8-0 Irish club ranked No. 2. Behind quarterback Joe Theismann, Ara Parseghian's imposing team was averaging over 540 yards per game offensively.

"They were so big," quipped LSU linebacker Richard Picou, "I thought someone had made a mistake and we were playing the Green Bay Packers."

But if Picou was impressed with Notre Dame, he didn't show it. He nailed an Irish ball carrier on a first down and goal from the LSU three-yard line, resulting in his second forced fumble of the game. Picou pounced on the ball to save a score.

But the stand that most remember came late in the game. All-American defensive back Tommy Casanova draped himself all over Theismann's key receiver, Tom Gatewood, and held the nation's second-leading receiver to just four first-half receptions and a paltry 21 yards. Late in the fourth quarter of the epic defensive struggle, with Notre Dame driving to a third down and goal at the LSU seven-yard line, Casanova stopped Gatewood yet again. As Theismann threw to his favorite target in the end zone, Casanova stepped in front of him and appeared to intercept the pass.

In what appeared as a prime example of the "Luck of the Irish," the ball slithered out of Casanova's hands, allowing Notre Dame to boot a 24-yard field goal and escape with a three-point win.

Even in the loss, eventual SEC champion LSU could claim credit. The performance was enough to secure a bid in the Orange Bowl, and because of the LSU defense, Theismann finished second to Jim Plunkett of Stanford in the Heisman voting.

Oddly enough, in the next week's AP poll, Notre Dame dropped to fourth, while LSU jumped a notch to No. 6.

October 24, 1970
"Anderson Does It Again"
LSU 17, Auburn 9

There's something about the Auburn series that seems to bring out the best in the LSU defense, and the 1970 Tigers were right in line with that tradition. Fresh off a tremendous goal-line stop of Auburn's Mickey Zofko in Baton Rouge in 1969, the LSU All-American linebacker repeated history on the Plains.

Auburn entertained LSU for the first time since 1908, and for this meeting, Shug Jordan's team was ready. The Plainsmen were 5-0 and ranked No. 6 in the nation, led by the aerial heroics of quarterback Pat Sullivan. Revenge for the 21-20 close shave the year before paramount in their minds, Auburn circled the LSU game on their calendars.

But Charlie McClendon's 4-1 Tigers had other plans. Thirteen-point underdogs, LSU took advantage of a muddy field and cobbled together a 17-9 fourth-quarter lead on touchdowns from Andy Hamilton and Art Cantrelle and a safety from Ronnie Estay, John Sage and Buddy Millican. But Sullivan marched Auburn to the Tiger three-yard line in the waning moments as he attempted to salvage a tie with a touchdown and a two-point conversion.

It was not to be. Sullivan audibled to an off-tackle play in an attempt to run between Sage and defensive end Art Davis, handing off to fullback Wallace Clark, his leading rusher. No sooner did Clark get the ball than Anderson roared through the hole and drilled Clark at the one-yard line to seal the victory.

"That was the finest one-on-one tackle I've ever seen," McClendon said after the game.

September 21, 1968 & October 8, 1966
"Tigers Stall Stallings"
LSU 13, Texas A&M 12
LSU 7, Texas A&M 7

Later in life, Gene Stallings discovered the secret to beating LSU, as he eventually posted a 6-1 record against the Tigers as the head coach at Alabama from 1990-96. But as a younger coach, Stallings tasted little but bitter disappointment in Tiger Stadium.

In 1966 and 1968, Stallings led talented Texas A&M teams into Death Valley looking for an early-season win. Both times he fell just short, and goal-line stands were instrumental in preventing his victory.

The 1966 game resulted in a 7-7 tie, but with less than 11 minutes remaining on the Tiger Stadium clock it didn't look like it would end that way. Sophomore quarterback Edd Hargett, who later played for the New Orleans Saints, engineered a fourth-quarter drive that threatened to give the Aggies a late lead. When a questionable pass-interference call gave A&M a first down and goal at the LSU one-yard line, the Tigers found themselves in a deep, deep hole.

Three dives to the middle later, however, the Aggies still had not moved. Linebacker Pop Neumann made two vicious tackles to bring up fourth and goal at the one-yard line.

Hargett waved frantically at Stallings on the sidelines to let him throw for a touchdown. But the coach ignored him, sending kicker Glynn Lindsey in for a 19-yard field goal attempt.

The kick sailed wide left.

"I should have listened to him," Stallings said. "I'd probably be better off."

LSU head coach Charlie McClendon called the goal-line stand "one of the best I've seen in a long time."

Two years later, the Tiger defense came up big in the fourth quarter to bite Stallings again. Defensive back Gerry Kent chased down Aggie runner Bob Long, stripping the ball at the LSU goal line and saving a touchdown as the ball rolled out of bounds in the end zone for a touchback. Kent's tackle preserved a 13-12 victory.

October 31, 1959 & November 1, 1958
"Show Stoppers"
LSU 7, Ole Miss 3
LSU 14, Ole Miss 0

It was the finest hour for LSU football, as a 1958 national championship and a 1959 Heisman Trophy for Bill Cannon sent the Tigers to the pinnacle of college football. And in that magical two-year period, a pair of classic victories over Johnny Vaught's Ole Miss Rebels stood out among the most memorable wins in LSU lore.

Naturally, the goal-line stand served as the ultimate weapon.

Most people think of Cannon's "Halloween Run" as the greatest play in the history of LSU football. While that may be so, the 89-yard punt return might not have even been the most dramatic play in the 1959 7-3 victory over Ole Miss. With less than a minute left on the clock, a Rebel drive set the ball at first and goal on the LSU seven-yard line. With mere seconds left, Ole Miss quarterback Doug Elmore rolled left on fourth and goal from inside the LSU one-yard line.

But a trio of LSU defenders, including Tiger quarterback Warren Rabb, swept over Elmore like a wave washing ashore and held Ole Miss out of the end zone to secure the victory.

A record crowd of 67,400 went wild, and the victory served as a springboard for Cannon's Heisman Trophy that year, as well as a sizable pro contract. The Rebels did get their revenge on LSU in the Sugar Bowl.

One of the most poignant factors in the 1959 stand was that it followed on the heels of the tremendous stand LSU made against the Rebels the year before.

With a scoreless game early in the second quarter of the 1958 match between the two powers, the Rebels faced first down and goal at the LSU two-yard line. Quarterback Bobby Franklin managed a yard on a keeper, and LSU was called off sides. In a costly fit of arrogance, the Rebels declined the penalty, sending the signal that they didn't need an extra down to score on the Tigers. But LSU center Max Fugler served as a bulwark to the Rebel advance, finishing a series of three tackles in four downs by shellacking Kent Lovelace for a one-yard loss on fourth and goal from the Tiger one-yard line.

The win vaulted LSU to national prominence, and indeed the national championship went the Tigers' way that year. But while Cannon got most of the credit, Fugler's performance in that goal-line stand was enough to put Tiger head coach Paul Dietzel in his corner.

"I wouldn't trade Fugler for any center in the nation," he said.

Paul Dietzel as coach. Courtesy of LSU Sports Information.

CHAPTER 3

Paul Dietzel

When you see Paul Dietzel, it's hard to imagine that the man is 77 years old. "Pepsodent Paul" could easily pass for much younger. It's also hard to believe that he was just 33 when he became LSU's head football coach in 1955, replacing Gaynell Tinsley.

Dietzel had remarkable football ties, having played at Miami of Ohio, the "Cradle of Coaches," as well as having coached there with Weeb Ewbank. He worked with Vince Lombardi at West Point while they were on the staff of Colonel Red Blaik. Additionally, Lou Holtz served as his assistant at South Carolina.

He won the 1958 national championship at LSU, where his staff included Charles McClendon, who later became the winningest head coach in Tigers history.

Getting the Job

A t Kentucky, Dietzel was the offensive line coach and McClendon the graduate assistant under Bear Bryant. Their wives, Ann and Dorothy Faye, were great friends.

"In our conversations, we always said whoever gets to be a head coach first is going to hire the other guy. As it turned out, I got the LSU job and Charlie Mac became my first assistant," Dietzel said.

Dietzel had an unusual connection to LSU that helped him get the job. The LSU coach from 1932-34 was Lawrence "Biff" Jones, whom Dietzel later got to know when he coached at West Point.

Dietzel graduated from Miami of Ohio in premed and was preparing to go to medical school at Columbia University. But yet another of Dietzel's remarkable coaching connections, Sid Gilman, called and asked him to coach the plebes at West Point. "The day I arrived at West Point was the day Biff Jones was retiring from the army," Dietzel recalled. "Biff went to Washington and handled the appointments for West Point cadets."

Dietzel, who took over Army's recruiting, talked to Jones on the phone three or four times a week. So when Gaynell Tinsley, who replaced Bernie Moore, left LSU, McClendon called Dietzel and told him to try for the LSU job.

"I told him, 'Mac, I don't even know where LSU is.' I had never been to Louisiana. He started naming off some of the Board of Supervisors. I didn't know any of those people. He said, 'Boy, oh, boy, if you knew someone who knew Biff Jones,'" Dietzel recalled with a smile.

"The next time I called Biff I explained what happened. He said he would call his friend Lewis Gottlieb, who was chairman of the board. Louis spoke for seven votes. He was a very powerful man and president of the City National Bank downtown."

Instead, Gottlieb tried to hire Jones back as LSU's coach or athletic director, but Jones wasn't interested and simply steered Gottlieb to Dietzel.

"That's how I got the job, and naturally, Charlie McClendon became my first assistant."

Governor, not Coach

Dietzel relates a story he heard about a time when Biff Jones was the LSU coach and the governor of Louisiana, Huey Long, thought he might do some coaching.

"Huey Long, along with his bodyguards, came down in the chute [at Tiger Stadium] and one of the bodyguards said the governor wanted to talk to the team," Dietzel said. "But Jones told Long's bodyguard, 'No one talks to the team but me.' And Long stomped off."

Dietzel said that Long told the LSU president, General Troy Middleton, to fire Jones, but that Jones had already taken a piece of paper, written down "I quit after this game," and put it in his pocket. Bernie Moore, who became an LSU legend himself, replaced Jones.

The Big Bucks

After a series of interviews, LSU offered the job to Dietzel for $12,500. "I said, 'Well, can you pay for my move down here?' Because we didn't have any money. They said, no, they couldn't do that, but they'd give me $13,000 to make up for it.

"I coached here for seven years and we had some pretty good years, especially the last four years, and when I left LSU I was making $18,000 a year. I had one perk: I had a television show on WBRZ and I got $1,000 for that. So my salary was $19,000 at LSU. I was born too soon. It's hard for me to relate to the salaries coaches make today."

Dietzel laughed and said that his wife, Ann, has told him he should come out of retirement and make a quick million.

"I just don't know anyone who wants to hire a 77-year-old football coach," he said with a smile. "But very frankly I think I could coach a lot better now. I learned a bunch of dumb things not to do again."

Getting Better

"You know, the first couple of years I was here we had a few good athletes but didn't have enough of them," Dietzel said. "There were other people who had more athletes than we did.

"There was a long spell in there where the downtown Third Street quarterbacks who kind of ran things wanted to get 'Greenhorn' back to West Point where he came from.

"And I got this wonderful letter from Gen. Troy Middleton, who was the president of LSU. It said, 'Dear Paul, I have heard there are rumblings on Third Street. And I just wanted you to know I like the way you're running our football program, and I am running this university.'

"Which is a wonderful pat on the back for some young coach, which I was at the time."

Things Got Better With a Backfield

LSU succeeded at recruiting Baton Rouge players, all keys to the 1958 title team. Dietzel was 3-5-2 in 1955, 3-7 in 1956 and only 5-5 in 1957. But in 1958, LSU had its first perfect season since 1908, finishing 11-0.

"That backfield had Billy Cannon, who was a fabulous athlete, Warren Rabb, who was a tremendous quarterback, and Johnny Robinson, who was about as good an athlete as you'd ever want to see. And when we got all this fine talent," Dietzel said, "it's amazing what a genius I became."

Start of Something Big?

When LSU won it all in 1958, did Dietzel think it was a once-in-a-lifetime happening for LSU or the start of something big? The Tigers have never come close since.

"I don't know. We started off that year not knowing how good we were," Dietzel said. "We played at Miami and [they] had a pretty good football team. That was the night everything kind of came together. We beat Miami 41-0 [to improve to 4-0] and I said, 'You know, we've got a pretty darn good football team.' Then things started building.

"But in order to have an undefeated football team, you have to have a lot of luck. It's impossible to have a team up for every single game. There are going to be games when you get by just because you're better than them. You can't play your greatest game every time. It's just impossible."

He smiled.

"That year we really destroyed Florida, 10-7," he said dryly. "And we beat the stew out of Mississippi State, which was one of the hardest teams for us to prepare for, because they were so physical, and we beat them 7-6. You have to have a lot of luck."

LSU's Three-Team System

"In my coaching career, I was the line coach for Sid Gillman at the University of Cincinnati. Sid went on to the Los Angeles Rams and the Chargers, and he was the one who invented the West Coast offense that everyone is talking about now in the pros. I was the defensive line coach for Sid and we practiced on the other field, because Sid believed in offense and all the good athletes were on the offensive team.

"Anyway, I was a big fan of [the comic strip] Terry and the Pirates. Milt Coniff was the artist. And in that strip there was a Dragon Lady and Chopstick Joe and so forth. Chopstick Joe said the Chinese bandits were the meanest and the most vicious people in the world. So I cut that out and put it on the bulletin board and said, 'From now on we're the Chinese Bandits.' Well, we had a pretty good team

Paul Dietzel as AD. Courtesy of LSU Sports Information.

and went to the Sun Bowl, but we had no national prominence at the University of Cincinnati.

"And then I went from there to Kentucky, where I was Bear Bryant's line coach, and then I went to West Point, where I was Col. [Red] Blaik's line coach."

The idea for the three teams at LSU came to him after a loss at Ole Miss in 1957.

"In the first half we had held our own," he said. But with Ole Miss platooning as many as three players in the second half, LSU was beat half to death.

"We made up our minds that we were going to have to develop [multiple] teams. We had a tough time getting two teams of equal strength. But we figured if we could put one team on offense, one team on defense and our best 11 would be the White Team, or starting team, we would play them the first half of every quarter and then platoon the other half of the quarter. Naturally the defensive team had to be the Chinese Bandits."

Can you imagine naming a unit as such in today's politically correct world?

"That wouldn't work any more, I don't think," Dietzel said with a laugh. "The Chinese Bandits, they weren't very big, [and] they were slow. Not a very good combination. But they proved to me what gang-tackling was. Because they were so slow they all got there at the same time. We always graded our athletes in every game on every play and if you weren't within a yard of the ball when the ball was ruled down you got a zero on the play. So they all arrived in a bad frame of mind and it made ball handlers get on the ground faster.

"At the end of the year, the best 11 on defense had allowed our opponents just under three yards a play, which meant in three plays they didn't get a first down. The Bandits allowed nine-tenths of a yard per play. And it proved to me it's morale over material three to one every time, as Napoleon said. But one of the greatest thrills I ever had in the coaching business was the Chinese Bandits."

Coaching with Lombardi

Vince Lombardi went on to fame as the head coach of the Green Bay Packers dynasty during the 1960s. A decade earlier, he was an assistant coach with

Dietzel at West Point. Dietzel was the offensive line coach, and Lombardi was the offensive backfield coach.

"We spent a year running the offense for the army. Vince Lombardi, I don't know if he was the smartest or the toughest, or the most organized person I ever saw, because I ran across some good ones. But I'll tell you that Vince Lombardi was the most intense coach I ever saw. He really was a marvelous fellow. He and Marie became really good friends of Ann and I. He went from Army to the New York Giants and then he went to Green Bay and became a legend."

Lou Holtz Credits Dietzel

L ou Holtz explained that Dietzel helped him overcome adversity. Dietzel brought his entire staff from Army and really didn't have room for Holtz.

"Show me anyone who is successful, and I'll show you someone who has overcome adversity. In 1966 I went to South Carolina as an assistant coach. My wife was eight months pregnant with our third child, and we spent every cent we had as a downpayment on a home," Holtz recalled.

"Paul Dietzel became the new head coach, but he kept only a couple of coaches off the previous staff. In my interview, he said, 'I'm going to do you a favor. I think you're in the wrong profession. We don't have a place for you. But we can put you in the P.E. department until the year is over.'

"I'm going to tell you, I was really downhearted and disappointed. But he called me in about a week later and told me, 'If you'll take a $4,000 salary cut, from $11,000 to $7,000, you can handle the academics and the scout squad,' which is what I did.

"Two years later I was at Ohio State with a team that won the national championship and a year after that I became head coach at William & Mary. It wasn't easy to hang in there back then, but I owe an awful lot to Paul Dietzel and to South Carolina."

But He Left

Dietzel said he would never leave LSU, a statement that came back to haunt him. Some LSU fans never forgave him.

"Keep in mind when I said those things, I was very young. And unless you have been around West Point, you don't understand what it's like. It was my very first coaching job. Col. Blaik was my hero. I was so impressed with West Point, which had never hired a civilian nongraduate. So I knew I could never go to West Point. And when I said that, I couldn't imagine there was any place I would rather coach than LSU. Everything about it I liked. I particularly liked the people.

"[At the end of the 1961 season], when West Point came calling, I really didn't know what to do. We had a great team coming back. In '62, '63 and '64, we had some great athletes. And I didn't know what to do. So I went in to see Jim Corbett, who was a fantastic athletic director, as was General Middleton a fantastic president."

Corbett reminded Dietzel he was under contract.

"I know that, and if you won't release me from the contract there's no point in me even talking to them," Dietzel told Corbett, who asked his coach what it would take to get him to stay.

"Jim, if I stay, I don't want an increase in salary, because I don't want people to think you paid me a lot more money to stay."

Corbett told him he would release him from the contract.

"Then we go play in the Orange Bowl in Miami and the night before the game I ran into Gen. Middleton."

Middleton invited Dietzel to his hotel room to chat and said that he knew he was talking to Army.

"He said, 'I'm surprised you haven't come to see me.' And I told him, 'General, I was really kind of embarrassed, but I was going to come to see you before I did anything.' Then he said to me, 'We really like you at LSU and don't want to lose you, but if West Point wants you to be their coach, you have to go. It's very clear, but you've got to go.'

"No one's heard that before, but as the Lord is my witness, that is exactly what he said. Gen. Middleton had some ties with West Point, too, of course."

His Return to Tiger Stadium

"This is really a goofy story," Dietzel said. "Jim Corbett called me in and told me we needed an opening game for 1966. He said there a lot of teams that will play us, but to pick out someone we could beat because the schedule was really tough.

"I said, 'How about South Carolina?' Well, I go to Army and [then] I go to South Carolina and guess what my first game is?"

Dietzel laughed, since the contract between LSU and South Carolina was signed in 1959.

"And I made up my mind that I didn't care how long it took, we were going to wait in the chute until LSU took the field. I didn't want our team to get intimidated by the crowd."

LSU won that game against its former coach, 28-12.

His Greatest Game

"**I**t had to be the Ole Miss game when we won 7-3 and Billy Cannon made that fantastic run," Dietzel said, recalling LSU's victory that included Cannon's remarkable 89-yard punt return on Halloween night in Tiger Stadium.

That run ensured that Cannon would win the Heisman Trophy.

"No athlete in America could have made that run, I don't believe. That was a very fantastic run.

"I have a picture that someone sent along a long time ago about the 15 finest football games ever played, and the LSU-Ole Miss game was one of them. And Johnny Vaught at Ole Miss was a very fine football coach, by the way."

Returning as Athletic Director

Charles McClendon was the LSU football coach, but despite his stellar record, many at LSU wanted him to go. Dietzel was considered as athletic director, and many thought he was brought in to fire McClendon.

"Before I came I asked the Board of Supervisors what the situation was with Charlie McClendon, because he was my friend," Dietzel recalled.

McClendon had 8-4 finishes in 1977 and 1978 but continued to lose to Alabama.

"I can't get involved in anything that's going to be embarrassing to either one of us," Dietzel said he told the LSU Board of Supervisors. "They said, 'Don't worry, that's all taken care of.' And so Charlie McClendon was coming up to be president of the College Football Coaches Association. I had to figure some way to keep him, so Charlie McClendon stayed at LSU for a year so he could be the president.

"I called Charlie and Dorothy Faye in and that's when I asked him, 'Charlie, have you and I ever had an argument?' He said 'No.' I said, 'Have we ever had a bad disagreement except for something like who should start at right guard or something?' He said 'No.'"

So Dietzel convinced McClendon to stay at LSU as his first assistant athletic director and announce his retirement ahead of time. Dietzel said he didn't fire his old friend, as many claim.

As it turned out, McClendon retired after the 1979 season and left anyway, heading to Orlando to run the Tangerine Bowl.

Life Now

Dietzel and his wife, Ann, split time between Beech Mountain, N. C., and Baton Rouge. He's become an accomplished watercolor artist, particularly proud of his painting of Tiger Stadium and how it looked in 1958. He calls it, "The Way We Were."

He loved to ski, but in his mid-60s Dietzel underwent a heart bypass.

"So I figured I'd better do something other than ski. I'd always had a yen to paint. So I took a few art lessons, and I really liked it. The only one I tried was watercolors. Everyone says that's the hardest medium. I don't know if it's hard or not, because that's the only one I do."

He has some of his paintings in a gallery. What's more, he's painted well over 150 pieces.

"I only have three or four left, so someone likes them," he said humbly.

CHAPTER 4

Steve Ward: Candid Recollections

Steve Ward, now a Baton Rouge State Farm agent, came to LSU in 1959 as part of the Tigers' great Baton Rouge connection of that era that included, just before him, Billy Cannon.

"I was deeply rooted in Baton Rouge. I grew up on Tecumseh Street in North Baton Rouge and we all kind of hung together. It was an us-against-them kind of world back then, across the tracks of Choctaw," Ward said.

Ward played at Istrouma High School and helped win two state titles in three years in a program that included Roy "Moonie" Winston just ahead of him.

"We all played together as little kids in elementary school, in the summers, into high school. We were teammates for life, almost," Ward recalled.

One of his best friends and high school teammates was Lynn Amedee. Ward, the halfback-linebacker, and Amedee, the quarterback-safety, made the most of their senior year in high school.

"Back then you could take as many trips as you wanted to. There were no limitations on trips," Ward said. "And after making All-State and prep All-American teams, we were getting recruiting letters from all over the country. So Lynn and I decided together to go see the country. We ended up seeing 10 or 12 different colleges. We'd leave on Fridays, come back on Sundays. Meet all the coaches, they'd wine and dine you, fix you up with cheerleaders, and they'd show you the campus and all that."

They went to Florida, Texas and Notre Dame, and Ward made a visit alone to Colorado. But they knew they were going to LSU the entire time. All the while, LSU assistant coach Charles McClendon was responsible for recruiting them.

"It got to be a couple of months after the signing date and Paul Dietzel started to get kind of nervous. And Coach Mac called and told us, 'You boys have got to sign pretty soon, because I'm under some heat.' The newspapers and all the fanfare said, 'Here are the two top players in Baton Rouge and in the South.' I didn't know if we were or not, but we were highly recruited and LSU hadn't signed us.

"Anyway, Coach Dietzel must have told Mac he wanted to meet with us.

"Once Dietzel visits your house and gets his feet under your kitchen table and gets your mom in there, you don't stand a chance. My mother was just enthralled with him. I

Steve Ward

Steve Ward. Courtesy of Steve Ward.

made that decision that night with the help of my parents: 'You're going to LSU!' And so we signed right after that."

Tough Defense

Ward played linebacker on the Chinese Bandits the first two years and then moved to the White Team. "I had fun when I played on the Bandits because it was what we did best. We practiced on defense and played one position on defense. We'd go in, kick ass, stop 'em and come off the field and watch the other team score a touchdown. Then we'd go back in and stop 'em. It was a lot of fun."

Freshman Wars

"I don't think there was a limit on scholarships back then. We got out there and they must have signed 50, 60 kids. Raymond Didier was the coach of the freshman team, and all we did was practice. I mean, we only had three games. It was really boring, beating against each other all the time. I wound up starting both ways as a freshman."

That group, which had a tremendous varsity career, included Jerry Stovall. The LSU freshmen went 3-0 in their games against other schools.

"But the worst part of being a freshman was playing in the Dust Bowl, the infamous Dust Bowl," Ward recalled. "We'd go to the practice field and they'd bring the guys who were redshirting and guys who dressed out but didn't play. The guys they were grooming for bigger and better things. They'd bring them over and we were meat for them. They'd been getting beat by the varsity all week long and they'd bring them over and say, 'OK, guys, here are the little freshmen, you can have them now.' I'll tell you one thing, as freshmen we were scared. They were grown men. We'd have the Dust Bowl every Monday, and I mean it was a war. All the varsity coaches, after they practiced on Monday, they'd come over and watch the Dust Bowl. Because they wanted to see how the redshirts and those guys were doing. They didn't care anything about the freshmen.

"We beat those guys one session on a Monday and you never heard more screaming and hollering from those varsity coaches. They just ragged those guys to death. From then on it was a war.

"The varsity coaches knew at that time we had an exceptional team."

Stovall, Ward, Field, and Soefker. Courtesy of Steve Ward.

Truly a Team

Ward emphasized that the team concept and the idea that the sum of the parts was greater than the whole were key for LSU as he rattled off the names of players he said were more or less average on their own but excelled when teamed with each other, like Bo Campbell, Jimmy Fields, Lynn Amedee, Fred David Miller, Billy Joe Booth and Bob Richards. "We were average to us, but outside looking in we had some damn good ballplayers. Nobody thought he was a superstar. Even Stovall wasn't a superstar when he first started. But he was the hardest worker on the team and put more effort into it."

Coming Into Their Own in 1960

"In 1960, we were all sophomores," Ward said. "In '59, Cannon and [the rest] left and in '60 Dietzel had to start from scratch. We played a lot of true sophomores. And in the first three or four games, we got our ass kicked. But we took our team up to Ole Miss and that's when they had Jake Gibbs and Billy Brewer, and we were kicking their ass. We had [about] 15 sophomore starters. They were supposed to win the national championship. We should have beat 'em. We missed an extra point and they kicked two field goals [to gain a 6-6 tie], and after that something clicked and we realized we were a damn good team. We only lost three or four more games the rest of our career at LSU. It's amazing how things click like that."

Thanks, Brother Ike

"**A**t Broussard Hall, we had restrictions that were tighter than the regular dormitories, but we had bourre [a Cajun card game] games on Friday nights with smoke billowing out of the rooms. We'd have five, six guys playing and smoking cigarettes, and Brother Ike, well, Brother Ike was a beautiful guy.

"Brother Ike was the dorm proctor. He was a beautiful guy. He'd come by for room check. He'd open the door and smoke would come billowing out, and he'd say, 'Just wanted to make sure you made room check.' Ike Mayeux, he was something. He was an older guy, but he lived at the dorm with his wife. He saw 'em come and go. But he kind of tolerated us.

"When we'd have an infraction, we'd have to go before the coaches and they'd break your plate, which meant they'd kick you off the training table for three or four days or a weekend. And they'd confine you to the dorm. They wouldn't let you go out on weekends. Usually it was for breaking curfew or something like that.

"Me and Sykes got caught out one time, and we got our plates broken for a week and we got confined to the dorm. Come Friday night and everybody's bailing out and Sykes and I are the only ones there. And old Brother Ike comes and knocks on the door. 'Hey, boys, you hungry? C'mon with me.'

"He took us to the kitchen, gave us a couple of gallons of ice cream, cooked a couple of steaks. He'd say, 'Don't you tell Coach, but I don't want my boys starving to death.' And he'd feed us like kings so we wound up eating more off the table than on it. But he was good to all of us."

At Florida

"**I** had a real good game. I was flying high, in the zone, intercepted two passes, we beat 'em in Gainesville. It was one of my highlights, intercepting two passes and leading the team in tackles."

LSU won the game 23-0 in Gainesville.

"You get in those zones and you have tunnel vision," Ward said. "You don't see or hear the crowd, you just go flying after everybody and go for the ball. Things slow down for you. You're at linebacker and you recognize and you're there before the play starts. The guard takes one step and you know what the play is. It's a trait you have that you don't know you have."

And On the Other Side...

"**W**e're playing Ole Miss [in 1962, a 15-7 loss], and they were kicking our butts. For some reason or another, we lost the edge and lost the focus. And it just seemed like they were coming at us. And they were getting ready to score, and in the huddle I'm just praying for an extra second to get another breath.

"In practice you practice your huddles, but in real life if you're tired you're tired. Well, I was calling defensive signals. Our signals were '50' or '50 Short' for [whichever] defense.

"Well, I'm sucking air and I did that," Ward said, putting his hand to his heart. "And everybody knew that if you did that you didn't have to say the defense. And here comes

Mike Morgan, a dear friend of mine who played for the Saints and who [has since] died.

"But he comes flying in there. He's a rookie and I'll never forget he has this clean, white jersey on and he comes prancing in there and he gets over in the huddle and everybody's dying, getting their ass kicked, blood flying, and he's in the huddle and I saw him and said, 'Damn, where'd you come from?' And he said, 'I'm here to play defensive end.'"

Ward imitated his own gasps and wheezed, "50."

"And he says, 'What's the defense, Steve? What's the defense?' And he tells the story after, 'Ward, I [came] in there and [looked] at you and you had snot hanging out your nose, blood dripping out your eyebrow, couldn't hardly see your face, and you were the meanest-looking sumbitch I'd ever seen.'

"And I told him not to do that to me ever again in the huddle."

LSU held the offense on that play, by the way.

Blue, Green

Ward recalled playing Georgia Tech at home in Baton Rouge.

"McClendon decided that since we had three teams we could put in two plays and wear them out. Blue and Green. Blue was a sweep to the left and Green was a sweep to the right. Blue because of B-L for left and Green for G-R for right. Idiots can remember that. All it was was toss sweep. Everybody from tackle to end went off running across the field. Georgia Tech just followed us across the field.

"But eventually we couldn't run anymore. We were just wore out. We had to call timeout to tell coach to stop calling that play. We were getting tired. Blue, Green, Blue, Green."

Big Money

At one time, the NCAA allowed a payment every two weeks to football players for laundry. The checks were for $15.

"If anybody ever spent a dime of that money on laundry it would have been a phenomenon," Ward said with a laugh. "It was beer money. At practice, when the checks came in, everybody was lining up like it was payroll checks."

Then many of them would head to Chris's Bar, an old place on 19th Street in Baton Rouge famous for its ice-cold beer in fishbowl-like mugs.

"We'd buy mugs till the money ran out. That was our laundry check."

Central Dietzel Time

"Coach Paul Dietzel was fanatical on organization, timing and being prompt. Playing under him was like being a plebe at West Point. I think he was deeply influenced by Red Blaik at Army. Everything we did at LSU was based on an itinerary with a time slot for everything. Every practice was timed to perfection.

"On game day, our itinerary would show us what we were doing from morning till kickoff. During pregame warmup, the team would file back into the locker room and get with their respective coaches for last-minute instructions. Well, there was a space on the itinerary allowing five minutes for 'NP.' As all players knew, we were allowed this time to take a 'Nervous Pee.' Coach Dietzel thought of everything!

"Another example of his obsession with scheduling and being on time was during preseason in the fall of 1961. We were going through three-a-days in August. It was hot as hell and were really beat up getting ready for the season opener. On his infamous itinerary sheet, he had a meeting scheduled for 1:05 p.m., which allowed the team to eat at noon and then have 35 minutes to go back to the room in Broussard and review our playbooks before the meeting. Well, I took a nap, and, as luck would have it, my alarm didn't go off. I awoke at one, according to my watch. My heart was pounding as I sprinted downstairs. I looked at my watch as I turned the doorknob to the meeting room, but it was locked. So I tapped on the door–lightly."

Ward was shocked as Dietzel himself opened the door.

"All 125 of my teammates were sitting in their desks totally silent. You could hear a pin drop. And I said, 'Coach, my watch shows it's 1:05.' Coach Dietzel looked at me with those steel gray eyes and said, 'Son, I don't recognize your time. I operate on Central Dietzel Time and you're three minutes late. See me after this meeting.'"

Ward had to run three miles after practice the next three days.

"I was never late again for any of Coach Dietzel's meetings, and to this day," Ward says with a laugh, "I still set my watch three minutes ahead and operate on Central Deitzel Time."

Shotgun

After each game, Dietzel's players had a 2 a.m. curfew. Making bed check was a priority. But that didn't keep the boys from hitting the Brown Door or Rip's Huddle, the latter owned by "every player's friend, Brother Schexnayder."

Ward said that on one particular Saturday night they made it back for bed check with no intention of staying. Making the rounds that night was speed coach Boots Garland.

"Boots would stick his head in the door, take one look at us, wink and say, 'Don't you boys get in any trouble later on tonight.'

"About five minutes later we'd start bailing out like drowning rats, going out the windows, flying down the stairs, whatever, and heading to the back parking lot, where frat brothers or girlfriends were waiting with their cars running."

They headed across the Mississippi River to Club Carousel.

"Most of us would get back before daylight, but on occasions one of our teammates would wind up in the Port Allen jail after a fight. And the sheriff would call Coach Dietzel to come get him. This would not be a good thing for the player."

Ward said different players got different punishments.

"If the player was a redshirt, he might be packing his bag and heading for home. If he was a starter, he might be packing his shoes for the stadium at 6 a.m. to commence running the north end zone steps until the next season. But if you can't do the time, don't do the crime!"

To Pick Cotton or Not?

After the 1961 season, LSU's bowl experience did not turn out as the players had envisioned, although the Tigers beat Colorado 25-7 in the Jan. 1, 1962 Orange Bowl. So in Ward's senior season, Charles McClendon's first season as head coach, the team wanted to discuss it before going to a bowl again.

"[In 1961], we worked our butts off in the prebowl workouts under Coach Dietzel and came to realize it was more like spring training than a reward to go to a bowl. Also, [us] single guys got the shaft at the Orange Bowl, because all the married guys on the team got to bring their wives.

"So we checked into the Fountainbleau Hotel in Miami Beach and the single guys looked around with that 'What do we now?' look. It was quite expansive on the strip and quite expensive, and we were quite broke. Anyway, to make a long story short, we found a couple of nice LSU fans who had more money than us and took in some of the sights that were not on the coaches' itinerary, if you get my drift. But we had to scrounge around to do it."

Fast forward almost a year, when bowl bids were coming out for the 1962 season.

"Coach got us together in the film room and was smiling from ear to ear. 'Fellas, we are invited to the Cotton Bowl and we're here to vote on it.' Well, little did Coach Mac know that we had gotten together before the meeting with all the single guys and voted not to go anywhere. Coach Mac almost had a heart attack when the show of hands indicated that the majority didn't want to go.

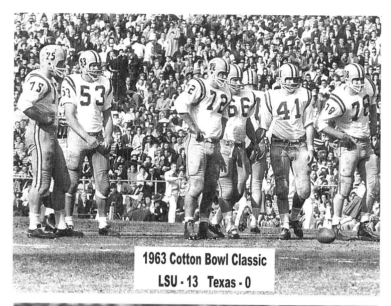

1963 Cotton Bowl Classic
LSU · 13   Texas · 0

Danny LeBlanc   Steve Ward

1963 Cotton Bowl Classic   LSU · 13   Texas · 0

Photos of 1963 Cotton Bowl Classic. Courtesy of Steve Ward.

"Fred Miller was our team captain and was chosen to meet with Coach Mac and [LSU athletic director] Jim Corbett to lay out our grievances."

The players, incredibly, demanded spending money and lighter prebowl practices.

"It must have worked," Ward said, "because [we] got a $250 'laundry check' before we left for Dalllas and we worked out in shorts and shoulder pads for most of the prebowl practices. And everybody was happy, because we beat Texas 13-0."

CHAPTER 5

More Big Hits

Extracurricular Activities

Football players constantly face the difficult task of balancing time spent on the playing and practice fields with time spent on hobbies and with loved ones. Some try to find time to go to dinner with a girlfriend, while some just want a little time to go to the movies or home for a good meal. Some, like former Tiger All-Americans Bert Jones and Tommy Casanova, just wanted to sneak away for some time in the outdoors.

In their case, the coaching staff discovered that football conflicted with good hunting and fishing time. Usually it wasn't a problem.

"I guess the NCAA would put you in jail for something like this now," said former Tiger receiver coach Jim Collier. "Bert and Tommy used to come out on Sundays and ask, 'Coach, can we borrow your boat? We want to go fishing.' They would get my little bateau and my little 9.8

horsepower Mercury and take off for False River with about 100 crickets to catch bream."

The perch-jerking was fine for the two during the spring, but like all good Louisiana outdoorsmen, Casanova and Jones were men for all seasons. When the fall rolled around, their thoughts turned to taking ducks on the wing or deer in the big woods, plans that often put them at odds with their coaches.

Bert Jones. Courtesy of LSU Sports Information.

"Casanova and I used to stand around the sidelines at practice and see all the wood ducks flying over," Jones said. "The practice fields were not too far from the Mississippi River and we knew those ducks were going to roost somewhere where there was a little swamp. So one day a buddy picked us up right after practice with the guns and the camo,

Tommy Casanova. Courtesy of LSU Sports Information.

and we followed those birds to where they were roosting and had, well, a really good hunt."

Casanova and Jones left the woods beaming about their accomplishment. But they ran into a bit of a problem when it came time to do something with their prizes.

"Both of us lived in the jock dorm, so we didn't really have a place to go with all of these dead ducks," Jones said. "We didn't think anyone would be there, so we decided to go back to the locker room at Tiger Stadium and clean them there. We were plucking and gutting ducks in the shower with the water running, and Coach Mac [Charles McClendon] came in and found us. We lost a few games during the course of my playing career at LSU, but I don't remember Coach Mac ever being as mad about any of them as he was about finding us cleaning ducks in the shower."

And There Were Deer

Ducks near the practice field were one thing, but according to Jones, they paled in comparison to the prize he calls "The Notre Dame Buck." Like many football fans, Jones struggled with the fact that football season and deer hunting season often butt heads.

"The weekend we played Notre Dame at home in '71 was the same weekend as the opening day of deer season in North Louisiana," Jones said. "All the guys on the team knew I was itching to go hunting. I really wanted to be in the woods. Well, we won the game and I thought I had all Sunday to get out of town and go deer hunting. But for what must have been the first time in history, Coach Mac called a team meeting for three o'clock Sunday afternoon. As soon as he said that, all the guys in the locker room looked at me and started laughing. They didn't think I'd be able to pull it off."

The thought of staying in Baton Rouge never crossed Jones's mind.

"I wasn't going to let some meeting keep me from hunting. So I went out and celebrated a little after the game, went home and slept for about an hour and a half and left Baton Rouge at about 2:30 a.m. for Ferriday."

Jones and good friend Brian Campbell arrived at Campbell's family's land just before sunrise. On the way from Baton Rouge, they mapped out a game plan to get Jones back to LSU in time for the team meeting.

"We figured we could hunt until 11:00 a.m., but not a minute after. We both took a stand before sunrise, and by 10:30 a.m. neither one of us had seen a thing. Brian went back to get the Jeep. He cranked the engine up about ten minutes till 11 and when he did, it scared a big deer that ran right to my stand. I shot the deer and fortunately it fell right where I shot it, because I didn't have even a minute to track it. It was a giant eight-point buck! We loaded it into the Jeep and dropped it off with a friend in Natchez on the way back, and I made to the meeting with not a minute to spare. Most of the guys on the team didn't believe my story, but I had pictures to show them later that week. I had the deer mounted, and it's still hanging on the wall in my office."

Say What?

All-American lineman Tyler Lafauci has an unusual Tiger Stadium memory of the first time he heard trash-talk.

"It was in 1972 against Ole Miss, the year we won 17-16. And Ben Williams, a big defensive tackle for Ole Miss who wound up playing with the Buffalo Bills, was a real competitive guy.

"In the beginning of the game all of a sudden he started mouthing off and talking. And we had never heard that in Tiger Stadium before. Never.

"At LSU, you played from when the ball was snapped until the whistle blew. You did your stuff and you got up and went back to the huddle. It was all business.

"But this guy was trash-talking me! Within myself, within the competitive nature of the game, it was funny to me. Because he was talking about my momma, he was talking about the LSU fans, all this stuff. I'd go back to the huddle and say to the guys, 'You hear what this guy's saying about your momma?'

"It was funny, but it was very intentional.

"During the last drive, he was still mouthing off. We got the ball back and started driving in the final minutes, and his trash-talking stopped. And the closer we got, the more nervous he got.

"On the last play, when [Bert] Jones threw the touchdown pass to [Brad] Davis and we scored, I was blocking on Williams. And I had him right under the shoulder pads.

"And when I realized we scored, I just lifted him and started trash-talking him. I threw him down on the ground and was just giving it to him."

Lafauci was laughing as he said, "And that was without realizing we still had to kick the extra point!"

Field Markings

Larry White, now assistant athletic director for sports information at Alabama, was a sports information director at LSU. He remembers a strange occurrence before LSU played host to Southern Cal in 1979, a 17-12 victory for the Trojans.

"That Friday some Southern Cal fans somehow got into the stadium," White recalled, "and with gasoline or something burned 'USC' into the northwest corner of the field. Nobody saw it till the next day. It wasn't big, but it was noticeable. The grounds crew had to go over to the practice field and cut a corresponding square out of the turf and bring it over."

Gridiron Club

The Gridiron Club is an LSU football group that once numbered as many as 600 fans. It now has about 300 members. The reason for the drop? Closed practices. When then-head coach Gerry DiNardo allowed Gridiron members into practice, the membership was bursting at the seams. But then he closed practices, and Nick Saban did, too.

The Gridiron Club is responsible for the remarkable annual event in Baton Rouge called the "Recruiting Bash," in which thousands of Tiger faithful gather on the first Wednesday of February for national signing day. The event, popular locally, has gained national attention and has become quite a happening.

The Gridiron Club was started in 1995 when Gerry DiNardo was LSU's football coach. He approached Bill "Chico" Moore, a Baton Rouge businessman and huge LSU fan. Moore's service station is a renowned place for LSU fans to hang out.

Moore said that DiNardo envisioned a fan group rivaling then-LSU baseball coach Skip Bertman's Coaches Committee.

DiNardo was the speaker at a monthly meeting of the Capital Area Tigers, a Baton Rouge fan group. After he left, Moore announced, "Coach DiNardo wants us to start a club like Skip Bertman's."

Within a couple of days, DiNardo had a meeting with Moore and some of his friends, including Vince DeSalvo and Ray Scimeca. The Gridiron Club was formed and the name was Johnny Schittone's idea. "And the rest is history," Moore said.

Art Cantrelle

In conversations with former players, one Tiger's name continually comes up as the toughest, baddest LSU player ever–running back Arthur Cantrelle, an All-SEC running back in 1970 and '71.

"He was just brought up differently," longtime LSU trainer Marty "Doc" Broussard said. "He could have been the heavyweight champion of the world. He weighed about 195. Tough. Goddamn tough. Anytime there was a tough situation, he would say, 'Give me the ball!'"

Former LSU quarterback Tommy Hodson said simply, "He was supposed to be the toughest bad-ass who ever played LSU football."

Art Cantrelle. Courtesy of LSU Sports Information.

To Shave or Not to Shave?

Players who were preparing to get married while still playing at LSU were subject to having their, well, groin area shaved. Such was the case for Art Cantrelle in 1971.

The team burst into his dorm room, expecting a battle. Cantrelle, evidently, just sat there quietly. An observer recalled, "He said, 'I'm going to let you do this. I'm not going to fight you. But I see everyone in this room. And I will get you one at a time.'

"Cantrelle is probably the only guy who got married with hair."

Tough Guy

Former LSU standout Lynn LeBlanc, who played on the 1958 national championship team and later coached at LSU, was a high school coach in the mid-1960s at the old Larose-Cutoff High School.

"Arthur Cantrelle was in about the eighth grade. We were going to need running backs the next year when he was going to be a ninth grader," LeBlanc said.

"I went to find him and went to the classroom. The teacher was gone and Arthur was up in front of the class, throwing erasers and chalk and teaching the class himself. I walked in and called him out in the hall."

LeBlanc told Cantrelle he thought he was good enough to play on the varsity the next year, but he had to clean up his act and hit the books. "I told him to pass and keep your nose clean. And Arthur, who had a habit of blinking his eyes," LeBlanc said, imitating the blinking, "told me, 'Yes, sir' and all that."

Cantrelle came out for spring practice, but something happened on the third day. "The next thing I know, he's arrested for whatever and he ends up at LTI [Louisiana Training Institute, an alternative school] in Monroe. Larose-Cutoff–where I coached and won the state championship in 1965–was going to consolidate with Golden Meadow and become South Lafourche [High School]. I had been appointed the head coach at the new school.

"Well, Arthur Cantrelle is still at LTI and I figured maybe we could get him back to South Lafourche."

But they traded places, in essence. LeBlanc took a job with Northeast Louisiana University in Monroe, while Cantrelle, did, in fact, make it back to play at South Lafourche.

"They ended up playing Broadmoor for the state championship," LeBlanc said. "Then he was too old, so he went to Biloxi High School because they could play at 19 in Mississippi."

A scholarship to LSU followed. "I got a chance to coach him, finally," LeBlanc said. "You know, Arthur, as tough as he was off the field–I know you've heard the stories–on the football field he was tough, but he was docile as could be. Three or four guys could hit him and he would blink his eyes and go back to the huddle. He wasn't mean as far as kicking people or slugging people on the football field. He did his job and was a very good football player."

Basketball vs. Football

Dale Brown coached the LSU basketball team for 25 years, from 1972-97. During that time, some of his Tigers played football, too, and he watched as seven coaches came and went: Charles McClendon, Bo Rein, Jerry Stovall, Bill Arnsparger, Mike Archer, Curley Hallman and Gerry DiNardo.

But there was only one with whom he almost got into a fistfight. It stemmed from an incident at the athletic dorm between members of the LSU football and basketball teams in 1992, during which Shaquille O'Neal put an end to things by knocking down football player Anthony Marshall.

"I got a call that there was a fight in the dorm and one of the football players had taken a pole or a two-by-four or something and was trying to hit one of the basketball players, and Shaquille intervened and knocked him down," Brown said.

"So I went up there, and it was a wild scene. They had dogs out there and they had police, and people were all over, and a guy was on the roof yelling obscenities. It was wild.

"The football players were taunting, 'We're going to get your All-American.' And they couldn't find Curley Hallman, so I told the assistants it was going to break out into something big if they weren't careful."

But it didn't end there. Brown nearly got arrested for arguing with a female plainclothes police officer on the scene. Brown questioned why she was there, she did the same about him, and they got into it.

"I apologized to her afterward," Brown said.

But not before Brown and Hallman met up later. "Curley insinuated that Shaquille started it. And you say things you shouldn't, but I said, 'You, a rookie, and you're going to come in here and tell me that?' And we had real strong words."

Which Dale Was Which?

In Curley Hallman's first year, LSU athletic director Joe Dean asked basketball coach Dale Brown to go on some speaking engagements with Hallman. The first was in Lake Charles.

"I didn't know anything about Curley Hallman except that he'd coached at Southern Miss and coached Brett Favre," Brown said.

"So he gets up to speak and I'm in the audience. He says, 'I was looking forward to today. Last night I was lying in bed with Dale...'

"And I'm thinking to myself, 'Is this a joke?'"

Hallman continued about how the night before he had asked Dale to get him a cookie, but was told he was getting fat.

"And I didn't know until then that Curley's wife was named Dale!"

Someone Call the Police ...

John Scarle, now a businessman in Baton Rouge and head of the "L" Club, was a football team manager. Some students didn't hit the books, but Scarle did. One of those times bred an incident in the library he'll never forget.

"We were getting ready to play Ole Miss, and I had a test coming up. There were some girls from the class who I was going to get some notes from in the Social Sciences department."

Scarle was sitting on the back of a chair and noticed it was pushed out a little differently than usual. Then one of the girls dropped a pencil and he bent down to pick it up.

"I saw there was some kind of grenade there, with something that looked like an airhorn.

"The reason I thought about the airhorn was because every day in practice I had to blow the horn when we changed periods. And this had a string tied from the airhorn to the chair, and it was pretty tight. So I knew what would happen if we moved the chair."

He tried to get one of the librarians to call the police, but instead got admonished for making too much noise. Finally they believed him and cleared the library.

The grenade was disarmed with him sitting atop it.

"November the third, 1972," Scarle recalled. "Scared me to death."

Gerry DiNardo. Courtesy of LSU Sports Information.

CHAPTER 6

Gerry DiNardo

Gerry DiNardo stands as one of the most compelling figures in LSU football history. He came on the scene and swept Louisiana off its feet with the "Bring Back the Magic" tour. The Tigers responded on the field, too, shaking off four losing seasons under Curley Hallman with winning years and victories in three consecutive bowl games.

But things went south the last two years of DiNardo's tenure as he battened down the hatches and sank into a "bunker mentality" that ultimately failed him.

DiNardo chose not to coach his last game at LSU, a victory over Arkansas in which Hal Hunter served as interim head coach. Instead, he kept a low profile before taking over as head coach of the Birmingham franchise of the ill-fated XFL.

Gerry DiNardo, an interesting and introspective man who prides himself on being college football's hardest worker, is now head coach at Indiana University, trying to turn that program around.

He was a most unlikely candidate for the LSU job. Joe Dean's account appears later in this book. What follows is DiNardo's perspective and insight into all the intrigue and behind-the-scenes drama that goes into hiring and firing an LSU football coach.

Finishing at Vanderbilt

The Vanderbilt Commodores were 5-5 and getting ready to play Tennessee when Joe Dean first inquired about DiNardo.

"I told him I was interested, but if I'm going to be one of the guys, I want to do it right away," DiNardo recalled.

Vandy got clobbered by Tennessee 65-0. At about the same time in Arkansas, LSU was beating the Razorbacks 30-12.

"[LSU sports information director] Herb Vincent, who heard I was a public-relations nightmare and didn't want anything to do with me getting the job, every time Tennessee scored another touchdown, Herb would keep giving Joe Dean the score: 35-nothing, 42-0, 55-nothing, like that, because he was trying to get me out of the picture."

Nonetheless, Dean met DiNardo the next day at the Marriott in Nashville.

"Before I sat down, I told Joe I appreciated him coming, but I never expected him to be here and we could just have something to eat and go our own way and I would understand. He interviewed me anyway, and we had a good visit. And he never said anything about the 65-nothing."

DiNardo drove Dean to the airport. "On the way he said, 'By the way, what did happen yesterday?' That was the first time he mentioned it."

Dean told DiNardo he would hear from him in a week, but no call came. By coincidence, the next week DiNardo was recruiting for Vandy in New Orleans and called Dean.

"He told me they were going to go in another direction, so he put me in the street. Interestingly enough, I [was] going to Baton Rouge to see Ryan Hebert at Catholic High School."

That night, while at the hotel in Baton Rouge, DiNardo got a phone call from an assistant in Nashville, who told him Dean was trying to find him.

"I called Joe. He says, 'Where are you?' I tell him I'm in Baton Rouge, and he says, 'Come on over, I want you to meet the president and continue the interview process.'

"I told him, 'No, you put me in the street already.' He said, 'I've changed my mind.' Well, I was in a sports jacket and tie, but not in a suit and I said I wasn't coming over."

They set up the appointment for two days later. In the meantime, DiNardo called his assistant back in Nashville and had him send a suit by overnight express and then went to Lafayette to continue recruiting for Vandy.

"I interviewed with Richard Gill [of the Tiger Athletic Foundation] and Charlie Weems [of the LSU Board of Supervisors]. Weems said he'd talked to some people in Nashville and heard I was a public-relations nightmare. I went and met with [President] Bud Davis and we had a lot in common because of Colorado."

DiNardo was a former assistant at Colorado and Davis was once interim head coach there.

"Joe Dean backed up into a student's car when we were pulling out, and we were being videoed by one of the local

TV stations in Baton Rouge," DiNardo said, laughing at the memory. "That was when I first learned that Joe was a nightmare driver. Obviously he had already driven his car into the lake at this time, but I didn't know it. But it was the tip of the iceberg. Anyway, he backed into a student's car that was parked by the chancellor's office. It was on video-tape. I started laughing.

"Then we went to the president's house, and Allen Copping says to me, 'Coach, if you're just interested in a raise, let's have lunch and we can send you back. We've gotten most of the other coaches in the country a raise. We can get you a raise also, but if you're interested in the job, let's talk.'"

Many coaches expressing interest in the LSU coaching job had parlayed that into a hefty salary boost from their own school.

"I thought that was an interesting way of starting a conversation. I assured him I was interested and not just trying to get a raise at Vanderbilt."

Nonetheless, DiNardo didn't think he was the leading candidate. "I kind of knew I was just like a token kind of interview or a backup. I didn't have a strong feeling I was going to get the job."

More Delays

Diardo then went to Ohio to do more recruiting and called Dean when he arrived.

"I called Joe when I got to the hotel and Joe says I'm out of [the running]. At which time I called [then-Vandy Athletic Director] Paul Hoolohan to tell him I'm out of the

LSU job, and he tells me, 'You've done irreparable damage on the Vanderbilt campus. I don't know that we can make this work anymore.' That wasn't a good day."

At the same time, LSU was offering the job to Texas Christian's head coach at the time, Pat Sullivan, the former Auburn star quarterback. But Sullivan had a buyout clause that neither he nor LSU could work out.

DiNardo then went to Florida to visit the home of Brent Bartholomew, who eventually played as a punter for Ohio State.

"His mother's a schoolteacher, and I'm sitting in their living room and selling them on the idea that there's only one school to go to in the Southeastern Conference if you really want an education and that's Vanderbilt."

On the drive home from the Nashville airport, DiNardo hears on the radio that the LSU press conference the next day had been cancelled.

"They were supposed to announce Pat Sullivan. As I was listening to the radio report, my wife calls me and says, 'Joe Dean called. He's got to talk to you right away.'

"I call Joe Dean from home and he says, 'I have to know if you'll take the job if I offer it to you tomorrow.' I tell him yes and he says he's going to work on it."

Dean called the next day to offer the job, which DiNardo took.

"By the way, two or three days later we called the Bartholomew kid back to see if he'd visit LSU. He wanted to, but then he cancelled."

DiNardo laughed.

"He said his mother wasn't comfortable with some of the things I said about the SEC other than Vanderbilt. Recruiting in a nutshell, right there."

Drive Home Safely

Dean called DiNardo the next day from a Board of Supervisors meeting in New Orleans and told him he was approved.

"Remember, we'd been in the car when he hit that student's car. By that time I'd heard a lot more stories about Joe's driving.

"He was on a mobile phone. I say, 'Joe, are you driving?' He says, 'No, why?' I said, 'Well, I don't want you to drive again till I have that contract in my hands.' He always tells that story. I think Herb Vincent was driving at the time."

The Great Comeback

LSU went 7-4-1 in DiNardo's first season, including a victory over Michigan State [coached by Nick Saban] in the Independence Bowl. During the off season, star running back Kevin Faulk got into trouble in his hometown of Carencro and was suspended for the 1996 season opener against Houston.

But in the weeks before that game, Faulk was reinstated.

"There were some conflicting reports on the police reports. There were some legitimate issues, and they weren't cleared up till late in the summer," DiNardo said.

Good thing, because he was instrumental in overcoming a 34-14 deficit at the beginning of the fourth quarter.

"We weren't playing very well for three quarters. Their defense wasn't very good, and Kevin ran back the first play of the fourth quarter, which happened to be a punt, and that got us in it a little bit," DiNardo recalled. "Then [offensive coordinator] Morris Watts found a soft spot in their defense and we started bringing the wing into the boundary. They never adjusted and couldn't defend it. We ran through them.

"Other than that, I'd like to tell you there was a time in that game when it all turned around, but other than Kevin's return there wasn't anything.

"I will tell you we had the best leadership of the years I was at LSU. We had Allen Stansberry on defense and Ben Bordelon on offense and they were probably the best captains we had."

Accordingly, asked later, DiNardo said those two players were his favorites from his five-year tenure at LSU.

DiNardo's Best Moments

"It would be hard to pick between the Auburn and Florida games," he said.

The 1995 Auburn game ended in a 12-6 victory on September 16 in Tiger Stadium, DiNardo's first at home as LSU's head coach. It marked big revenge for LSU, because the Tigers lost at Auburn the year before in the game that will always be remembered for quarterback Jamie Howard's four interceptions.

"It was the first time LSU had worn white jerseys in 18 years, and we had worked hard to get that done. And they were sixth in the country. I just think it got our program off [to a good start]. We were 1-1 on the road and came back and won that game at home.

"And then the Florida game was fun. That was a good game."

The "Florida game" was LSU's 28-21 upset of the No. 1 Gators on October 11, 1997, a victory that produced seemingly a million commemorative T-shirts and helped recruiting for years to come.

Funny to note are the remarks DiNardo gave the team and the media before that contest.

"I told the team, 'Don't listen to what I tell the media this week.' One thing I said intentionally was wondering which open receiver Florida would throw the ball to. ESPN did a piece on the game and made fun of that. I think they called it DiNardo doing his best Lou Holtz."

The Color Purple and Steve Spurrier

The next summer DiNardo and his wife, Terri, met up with the Spurriers on a Nike-sponsored trip to Hawaii.

"At dinner, Steve says 'Gerry, you guys are way too good and mean when you wear those white shirts. I'm going to make you wear purple when you come to Gainesville.' My wife, Terri, says, 'Steve, we can wear pink. We're still going to beat you!' And I look at her and..." DiNardo shook his head.

Referring to the next year in Gainesville, DiNardo said, "I wouldn't wear purple. We wore gold." And LSU lost 22-10 in a game that with a couple of breaks—including not dropping two wide-open interceptions—could easily have been a Tigers victory.

Kennison Gone

"When Eddie Kennison scored that one touchdown [against Michigan State in the 1995 Independence Bowl] and hopped the fence," DiNardo recalled, "I turned to someone on the sideline and said, 'He's leaving for the NFL this year. That was like a gazillion-dollar jump.'"

DiNardo's Worst Moment

"The [1999] Kentucky game, we didn't play well. The other thing about that game was that [the Tiger Athletic Foundation's Richard] Gill and all the boys were supposedly talking to [UK coach Hal] Mumme about the job. So that wasn't any fun. They all deserve one another; it just didn't happen."

LSU lost that game 31-5, but bounced back the next week to beat Mississippi State 41-6. But after that, the Tigers lost three in a row and sealed DiNardo's fate.

Tough Times

LSU was 3-0 to start the 1998 season and was ranked No. 6 in the country. Early in the fourth game, against Georgia in Tiger Stadium, the Tigers faced first and goal from the five-yard line.

Al Jackson jumped off sides and marked the beginning of the end. Georgia's Champ Bailey and Quincy Carter had career nights in a 28-27 victory. LSU would only win one more the rest of the season.

"I don't know that there was much of a reason [why we had such a poor season], other than it was part of the game," DiNardo said. "We lost tough games. Kentucky was better than it had been. They had [QB Tim] Couch, the first pick in the [NFL] draft. Obviously we know now that most of Kentucky's success was more due to Couch than anything else. Remember that game with the reverse at the end? I just think it was football."

DiNardo's Tigers did have some more bright spots during the season. "We beat Mississippi State that year 41-6 and they went to the championship game. We played Florida and it was 6-3 at halftime.

"I don't know what it was. We lost our defensive coordinator [Carl Reese] and we were already in transition defensively. And then the next year we were in transition offensively."

Before DiNardo's fourth season, defensive coordinator Lou Tepper took more than his share of heat for the Tigers' failures, especially in the backfield.

"Lou Tepper came into my office and volunteered to resign. I told him no, it wasn't his fault, he'd done a good job with the defense. We just lost some players."

Before the fifth year, however, athletic director Joe Dean told DiNardo that it would be touch and go.

DiNardo told Dean that he wanted LSU chancellor Mark Emmert to agree that if his record was not up to par midway through his sixth season, he would resign. But Dean did not agree that that was the best way to handle the situation.

The Strange Time with Master P

The fabulously rich and famous rap artist Master P, aka Percy Miller, moved to Baton Rouge and immediately became a factor on the scene. He befriended athletes from LSU and crosstown school Southern University, and observers feared NCAA violations and a power play between the rapper and the coaches.

"I don't know how much he was involved, or if he even was. I actually think people were unfair to him in assuming that he was part of the problem. He may have been, but I don't know," DiNardo said.

"I don't follow rap music. I have nothing against him. I don't know what involvement he had, if any. I had no reason to think it was an issue."

Nonetheless, rumors always persisted that Master P bought his friendships with LSU athletes.

"I don't know if he had any impact on what we were doing," DiNardo said.

The two never met, according to DiNardo, despite talk to the contrary.

"I offered to meet with him, but at the time I had the same stance as I had now. I didn't know what I was going to say to him, but I did offer to meet with him."

At the End

When DiNardo got his walking papers after five years, he had one request. "I asked them for a half-hour to tell my family. My daughter was at Notre Dame.

Michael was in school and my wife, obviously, was at home. I wanted to tell them first before they heard it on the news.

"I hugged Joe and thanked him. Joe obviously was against it and he told me that in the meeting, in front of [Chancellor Mark] Emmert, and I appreciated that a lot.

"I walked out of the alumni center, and I called Terri and told her we just got fired. So we met for lunch. A bunch of people were looking at us and wondering what we were doing there. And that was it."

The Rotary Debacle

DiNardo was adamantly against making speeches or outside appearances from the moment practice began through the end of the season. That didn't help him at the end, especially not with the Baton Rouge Rotary, one of the most prestigious organizations in the city.

"The Rotary guy in charge routinely calls my office and my secretary tells him I'm not available that week because we're back into football. Anyway, I get the guy on the phone and tell him that I know I've done it before, but it's just a bad time and I just don't want to do it this year. He tells me they'll miss me and I tell him I appreciate that, but just want a year off.

"I [would have had to] prepare for that. They video it and they play it on that [Baton Rouge TV] station, so you can't just go there and wing it. It takes some time to prepare and I didn't want to do it.

"What I didn't know was that the guy I talked to was calling people around town to apply pressure for me to speak, including [President Bill] Jenkins. The next thing I know,

Joe Dean's calling me, asking why I wasn't speaking at the Rotary.

"And I said, 'My goodness, just because I don't want to.' Joe says, 'The president really thinks you should.' The president? It's that important to them? And Joe says, 'They say every football coach speaks there every year.'

"I tell him, 'That's true Joe, but there's been no football coach who's spoken there more than four years in a row because nobody lasts more than four years. So this is the year I would have had off anyway. I would have been fired.'

"So Joe thought it was funny. Then I told Joe if it's that important to Jenkins I'll resign. If he's going to make me speak at the Rotary, I'll resign the position as head football coach at LSU."

Stubborn to the end, DiNardo held fast.

"I always say that me not speaking at the Rotary was one of the reasons I got fired at LSU."

Bitter Memories

"When I think of LSU football I think of bitterness, probably. For me," DiNardo said in the spring of 2002 on a walk through the Indiana campus.

"Most of us end in crash landings. You can't find a picture of Bobby Knight on this campus, and he's won three national championships. That's pretty typical of how this business ends. Very few people leave any university without bitterness. Nick [Saban] will leave bitter. People will either be bitter toward you or you'll be bitter toward them. If he gets fired he'll be bitter. If he leaves, people will be bitter towards him.

"When was the last time any of these relationships did not end with bitterness on one side or the other? You'd be hard-pressed to find one."

CHAPTER 7

LSU Mascots

Just how many "Mike the Tigers" have there been? How did LSU get Mike? What mascots did the Old War Skule have before Mike? "Little Eat 'Em Up" ring a bell? As the Tiger Athletic Foundation launched a full-scale effort in 2002 to build Mike a new home–a Tiger habitat, if you will–could there be a better time to uncover the myth of Mike?

Many facts regarding the history of Mike the Tiger are shrouded in mystery. Two members of the LSU Department of Biological and Agricultural Engineering, Andrea Albright and Marybeth Lima, wanted to clear things up. They admit they weren't totally successful, but they had fun doing the project, and their efforts to provide an integrated, comprehensive history of mascots at LSU go a long way. Their research is much appreciated.

A Live Tiger

The use of live animal mascots at American universities peaked in the first part of the 20th century. Following the lead of schools such as Princeton University and Columbia University, LSU got a live tiger in 1936 for the first time. Princeton's live tiger mascot of the early 1930s is believed to be the first such mascot in the nation.

Columbia's lion, which the school acquired in the 1920s, still enjoys notoriety today. He is the roaring lion that appears on all MGM films. Today most schools have discontinued the tradition of owning exotic animals as mascots. Besides Mike the Tiger, the only other live tiger mascot in the country today is TOM at the University of Memphis. TOM, whose name is an acronym for "Tigers of Memphis," is Mike's full brother.

Mascots Before Mike

During the Civil War, at the battle of Gettysburg, a brigade of Louisiana soldiers led by Captain Harry Hays charged up Cemetery Ridge and subdued the Union artillery stationed there. Because of their ferocity in battle, these soldiers became known as "Louisiana Tigers." Among the members of the battalion were many LSU cadets and professors, including David French Boyd, who became LSU president after the war.

In 1893, the first football team at LSU was formed. The team chose the tiger as its mascot in honor of the Civil War's Louisiana Tigers. Although tigers were associated with

LSU's football team from the beginning, many years passed before a live tiger was actually used as a mascot. A dog that was included in the 1896 LSU football team photo may have been the first mascot.

A few years later, a young boy, David Reymond, appeared in the 1908 team photo and is listed as the mascot. Several other boys were pictured in team photos around the turn of the 20th century. What duties these mascots had, if any, is unclear.

The first big cat mascot was introduced to the LSU community in 1924. That year, "Wild" Bill Graham, an LSU student fond of adventure, took a trip to South America. During his travels, he acquired a jaguar (also known as a black bob-tailed tiger), which he brought back to LSU to serve as the mascot. However, the cat, nicknamed "Little Eat 'Em Up," was not a great success with LSU fans. Reports say that he had a habit of turning his back on the action and cowering just when the football team was about to score a touchdown. LSU did not win a single major game during the 1924 season, and "Little Eat 'Em Up" was deposed. His specific fate is a mystery, but LSU fans never saw him again.

"Short-stride" and the "Vegetable Man"

In the absence of a live mascot, fans of the 1920s and '30s used papier-mâché tigers as symbols of school spirit. Made of paper, plaster and paint, these handsized to life-sized sculptures of tigers rode to games on the hoods of cars or were held up on poles by fans in the stands.

In the years immediately preceding Mike the Tiger's arrival on campus, the LSU football team had two addi-

Eddie with Piglet. Courtesy of Marybeth Lima and Jim Fiser.

tional human mascots. One was an African-American teenager named Johnny "Short-stride" Tinsley Thomas, Jr. The football players scratched his head for luck before each game, and he sat on the bench with the team during games.

An extensive literature search yielded little information about the length of Johnny's tenure as mascot. He was officially listed as an LSU mascot in 1936 and was pictured in one issue of *Gumbo*, the LSU yearbook. He was not listed in the 1930-1950 Baton Rouge Census. A local community member who remembered Johnny thought he went to California just after World War II, but no definitive information is available. At the present time, the story of Johnny "Short-stride" Tinsley Thomas Jr. remains a mystery.

The same year that the school acquired Mike, LSU hired a spirited public figure known in Baton Rouge as "Eddie the Educated Vegetable Man." Eddie acted as a combination mascot, cheerleader, and parade leader. Like Johnny, Eddie was an African-American, and his real name was Porter Bryant. He made his living selling vegetables that he grew on the site of the old LSU football field in what is now downtown Baton Rouge (LSU moved to its present location in 1925). Eddie called his harvest "educated vegetables" because of where he grew them. He sold them daily from a pushcart in downtown Baton Rouge, yelling his famous sales pitch, "Get your educated vegetables here!"

He also had an ice cream vending business at LSU, but a 1936 vendor's law pushed him off campus and out of business. In response, the LSU student council invited Eddie back to LSU to serve in the capacity of mascot, as Eddie was well known as a devout LSU football fan. Eddie accepted this position and later became Mike the Tiger's first keeper. Eddie also led the Tiger Marching Band onto the football field at halftime.

Mike I

Although no one intended to keep the date of the first Mike's arrival a secret, it is impossible to claim with certainty exactly when the tiger made his debut on campus. The 1936-37 edition of *Gumbo* gives November 21, 1936 as the date of Mike's arrival, but official records and newspaper articles report that Mike first left his paw prints on campus October 21 or 23, 1936. A photograph taken at the 1936 LSU-Arkansas game on October 24, 1936 proves that the November date is incorrect. Eddie the Educated Vegetable Man was pictured standing in front of Mike's traveling cage (with Mike inside), holding a piglet.

LSU pranksters gave Eddie the piglet, presumably symbolic of the Arkansas Razorbacks' mascot (word has it that the piglet was returned to its rightful owner and not fed to Mike). The picture could have been taken only at the 1936 game, because LSU did not play Arkansas again until 1946, by which time Eddie had passed away.

Although the exact date remains unidentified, we know for certain that the name "Mike the Tiger" was first heard on campus in the fall of 1936. According to the 1937 edition of *Gumbo*, the first person to suggest using a live tiger as mascot was Mike Chambers, a popular trainer for the football team. The student body quickly took up the idea of a live tiger mascot.

"We wanted a mascot that could stand up and roar," explained Jack Fiser, a student at LSU in 1936. Another student, Ken Kavanaugh, who would later become a football All-American, told Mike Chambers that three tiger cubs had recently been born at the Little Rock Zoo in Arkansas. With that announcement, what can only be described as a tidal wave of enthusiasm for the new mascot began. First-year law student Eddie Laborde, a friend of Kavanaugh's, was instrumental in bringing Mike to campus.

Eddie was in the gym armory shaving the heads of freshmen when Kavanaugh approached him and said that he knew where they could get a tiger cub. Kavanaugh's father was the zookeeper at the Little Rock Zoo and had a tiger cub named Sheik, who had been born a few months earlier, on October 8, 1935.

Eddie organized a fundraiser and asked each student to contribute a quarter to buy the mascot. LSU students rose to the occasion in true tiger spirit. Within an hour, they raised the $750 needed to purchase the tiger, quite a feat considering that America was suffering in the depths of the Great Depression at the time. When they had enough to purchase the cub, Eddie and Ken arranged to have him sent from Little Rock.

When dawn broke on the day of the tiger's arrival, pandemonium ensued. Students declared a holiday (without the consent of the administration), and the cadet corps gathered at the campus gates before sunrise to turn away professors and students with books. Picketing students broke up classes, and people milled all over campus. The cub was scheduled to arrive by train at the downtown train station, but because of the size of the crowd gathering there, city and university officials made a quick change of plans. They rerouted the confusion onto campus, where, even if it couldn't be controlled, at least it wouldn't disrupt downtown traffic.

City and state dignitaries were present for the occasion, and Eddie the Educated Vegetable Man showed up at the LSU station to declare himself keeper of the new mascot. The train pulled into the crowded campus station several hours late, with the conductor yelling, "We've got the tiger!"

"I thought he'd be a pussycat," Eddie said, expecting to see a cub. "Instead of being six inches long, he was six feet long!"

Eddie and others took control of the tiger with the assistance of popular football trainer Mike Chambers. They placed him in a wheeled cage made by Commissioner Wendt of the Highway Department. Luckily, Mike Chambers had previously worked with Ringling Brothers Circus and knew how to handle the cat. For this reason, and for his popularity, students yelled "Mike!" when asked what the tiger should be named.

At noon, administrators declared the day an official holiday. Mike the Tiger was placed in his traveling cage and led a parade going the wrong way down Third Street (a one-way street near campus), which was the traditional way to celebrate great events at LSU. The excitement over Mike the Tiger was just beginning. The entire campus celebrated with dances and bonfires well into the night. The day Mike the Tiger arrived at LSU quickly became legendary and is still a part of LSU lore.

Several days later, Eddie and others took Mike the Tiger to Shreveport for the annual football game with the Arkansas Razorbacks. Along the way, they collected money to pay for Mike's daily ration of 19 pounds of meat. Eddie Laborde, along with Hickey Higginbotham (the LSU swim coach, who also played a major role in Mike I's life), "Boomin'" Carney and Eddie the Educated Vegetable man, exhibited Mike to students at schools between Baton Rouge and Shreveport and collected their lunch money to feed the cat. Laborde recalled that they bought meat for the tiger at a Jewish Deli.

"We had to pay extra because we were gentiles," he reported.

The LSU tigers, with Mike as their mascot, beat Arkansas 19-7.

Mike Gets to Stay

When they boarded the ferryboat to cross the Mississippi on the return trip, surprisingly, the Governor of Louisiana boarded just after them. Governor Richard W. Leche saw Laborde with the tiger cage and approached him with these words, "Are you the boy responsible for that tiger?"

"Yes, sir, I am," Eddie responded.

"Well, what are you gonna do with him now that you got him?"

Eddie's plans were vague. He told the governor that he had a cousin who worked at City Park Zoo in Baton Rouge;

the cousin said that there was a very sick lion at the zoo, and if the lion died, Mike could have his cage.

"You come see me first thing Monday morning," was the governor's response.

The governor told him to be there at nine. Eddie was there at eight. The governor said he could get money from President Roosevelt to build the cage, and he did. The original cage (part of which still stands) was financed by a WPA (Works Progress Administration) grant, as a part of President Roosevelt's public works project. The ceremonies for the dedication of the cage were held on April 13, 1937.

Although Eddie Laborde views his experiences with Mike the Tiger as some of his fondest memories, his involvement with the tiger distracted him from his class work. When he showed up in one of his law classes after a two-week absence, the instructor, Mrs. Harriet Daggett, expressed surprise at his presence and told him that the dean wanted to see him.

Eddie's account of his conversation with Dean Frederick K. Beutel of the Law School follows:

Dean: "Where have you been?"

Eddie: "I've been messin' with this tiger for a couple of weeks."

Dean: "Yes, I heard about that tiger. They [the students] almost turned my car over at the gates on the day he arrived. I don't think you're going to be able to make up your work. You'll have to find another college."

Eddie: "But I've already been in every college on campus except Agriculture, and I'm not going to be a farmer."

Dean: "Well, you're not going to stay in my law school."

Thus, the law student partially responsible for bringing the first tiger to LSU unceremoniously left the university.

Mike the Tiger lived his first six months as a mascot in a cage at Baton Rouge City Park Zoo while a new home was built for him on the grounds of LSU. Mike's campus home consisted of a 12-by-15-foot stone building and an adjoining outer cage of slightly bigger size. The stone portion of the cage, also called the "winter cage" is still a part of the current cage. In all, the original cage offered him approximately 600 square feet for living quarters. As one writer for the *Reveille*, the campus newspaper, said, the cage became "a Mecca for campus visitors."

The new mascot, as part of his main duties, attended LSU football games to boost team spirit. In the early days, Mike attended both home and away games, but after an automobile accident in 1951, he stopped making road trips. Whether home or away, Mike was wheeled around the stadium in his traveling cage, inspiring cheers from LSU fans and, hopefully, striking fear into the hearts of the opposing team. It was common practice to poke at Mike with sticks or poles to get him to roar at games because supposedly the number of roars predicted the number of touchdowns the football team would score.

In his years on the LSU campus, Mike I took part in a few notable adventures. In 1943, he experienced the effects of the Second World War. LSU officials could not procure enough meat to feed Mike due to meat rationing imposed because of the war, and therefore transferred the tiger to the New Orleans Zoo. In March of 1943, a *Reveille* writer reported that Mike's usual daily diet of ten pounds of steak (donated by a local company) had been replaced by the same amount of "scrap beef." A month later, the Baton Rouge *State-Times* reported that "there are no provisions for pets included in the rationing regulations, and he [Mike] could only get horse meat and cereal."

In the same article, university officials stated that Mike was sent to New Orleans so that he would be ensured proper food and care for the duration of the war. Audubon Zoo had several thousand pounds of meat in cold storage, and Mike shared this bounty.

Unfortunately for the well-meaning administrators, the student body was not at all receptive to the idea of sending Mike to New Orleans, the home of their greatest football rival, Tulane University. On the day of Mike's scheduled departure, protesting students kidnapped student body president Hugh O'Connnor and vice president Jeff Burkett, locked them in Mike's traveling cage, and pushed them around campus. After this and other protests, the administration relented and allowed students to vote by mail or phone ballots on the issue four days later. During this time, the official reason for sending Mike to Audubon Zoo changed. Administrators explained that Mike was being sent away for breeding because he was getting old and needed heirs. Mike was eight years old, and the average life expectancy for a tiger at that time was twelve years.

Coach Higginbotham said, "I am on as close terms with Mike as possible, and he's soon going to curl up and die." Mike, he said, was "worth his weight in gold to LSU," and argued that breeding him was the only logical thing to do. When given this reason, the students agreed to let Mike go, and he left campus three days later. Mike never produced any heirs. He returned home after the war, but unfortunately Eddie the Educated Vegetable Man was no longer there to greet him. In 1945, Eddie stepped on a nail and became critically ill with lockjaw. Shortly afterwards, he died of pneumonia. News of his death ran in the September 26, 1945, edition of the *State-Times*.

In 1950, Mike and the LSU community were subjected to one of the most humiliating events of this mascot's, or any of his successors', careers. While Mike was en route to New Orleans for a football game against Tulane, he was kidnapped, or catnapped, by Tulane students, in what was, according to his student keeper, a well-orchestrated plot. The keeper, David Melilli, claimed that "the stealing of Mike was well planned and not just a spur of the moment idea."

Whatever the case, LSU fans saw red when their beloved mascot was wheeled onto the field just before the game, in a cage painted Tulane green. LSU fans will agree that the Tigers brought about a piece of poetic justice when they managed to tie the highly favored Tulane team 14-14.

Mike I earned a reputation for his fierceness and viciousness. Despite an unfriendly temperament, Mike did have qualities that endeared him to the LSU faithful. One of his most widely known character traits was that he never ate in front of people.

On Mike's 13th birthday, a newspaper photographer waited for hours to get a shot of Mike eating a tiger-size birthday cake that his keepers had placed in his cage. Even though the cake was topped with hot dogs instead of candles, it seemed to be of no interest to Mike. Frustrated, the photographer finally gave up and packed up his tripod and camera. As he walked away, he turned back and saw Mike, the winner of the showdown, munching on his cake.

Mike I also gained fame for roaring without being prompted. During his twilight years, he graced the ears of whoever would listen with roars at regular half-hour intervals.

The first Mike lived for over 20 years and was the oldest captive tiger on record when he died. Like the date of his arrival, the date of Mike's death is also a point of contention. A small minority maintains that Mike died in 1957, during an LSU football losing streak. However, unlike Mike's arrival on campus, clear documentation exists to show that Mike's death occurred before the infamous losing streak. He died on June 28, 1956 of an acute kidney infection.

Mike II

The search for a succecessor to Mike I began almost immediately after his death. While students in mourning draped pictures with black cloth and raised money to have the mascot stuffed, administrators contacted

Mike II. Courtesy of LSU, University Relations.

zoos to see if a new cub could be purchased. Mourners were successful in getting Mike I stuffed; he is still on exhibit at LSU's Foster Hall.

Administrators were also successful; they found the tiger that would become Mike the Second at Audubon Zoo in New Orleans. Zoo superintendent George Douglass arranged for the cub's transfer through correspondence with LSU officials. Students, alumni and friends of LSU raised $1,500 to pay for the tiger.

The new Mike made the trip from New Orleans to Baton Rouge in the back seat of Mrs. George Douglass's Cadillac on September 28, 1956, the seven-month anniversary of his birth. The day after he arrived, LSU's second tiger mascot was officially introduced to the student body.

Twenty years after he left campus, Eddie Laborde got a phone call from General Troy H. Middleton, the commandant of cadets. The general delivered the news of Mike the Tiger's death with these words: "Your tiger died. They got a new one, and they want you to put it in the cage." Eddie flew from his home in Alberta, Canada, and was at LSU the next day.

This time, the administration sanctioned the celebration, and a parade in honor of Mike II wound its way through campus and the surrounding areas, led by Mike Chambers and Eddie Laborde. Before the day ended, little Mike II was whisked away to his inner cage to protect him from the stress of his new environment. Joe Dixon, the veterinarian in charge of Mike, explained that the cub would need time to adjust to his new surroundings.

"He will probably spend his early days just hiding out," Dixon said. Mike emerged from his new home that evening to attend the first football game of the season against Texas A&M. He was brought into the stadium, introduced a few minutes before kickoff, and returned to the cage.

Several weeks after Mike II arrived, athletic director Jim Corbett reported to the LSU community that the cub was having difficulty with the crowds and the stress of being on display. Corbett and Dixon decided to confine him to his den without public display for a month, to give him time to adjust.

On February 28, 1957, an article entitled "Corbett Dispels Tiger Death Tale" appeared in the *Reveille*. The article responded to rumors circulating the LSU community claiming that Mike II died while in his cage and was replaced with another tiger. The reporter wrote, "Rumors are flying that Mike II died a few months ago, but a *Reveille* investigation has proven that statement to be a falsehood."

The rumors apparently started because several people noticed a large weight increase between the tiger that went into seclusion and the tiger that came out. The article went on to state, "Athletic Director Jim Corbett staunchly denies that poor Mike has taken a trip to the beyond." Corbett admitted that Mike II had, indeed, encountered difficulties adjusting to his new home. The reporter wrote, "Corbett added that when Mike was first brought here in September, he had a couple of 'convulsions' and was jumping around all the time because he was not used to the people around him. It was then that the veterinarian in charge of Mike recommended that he be kept under cover in the cage for a few weeks."

Eventually, the rumors ceased. For 40 years, no one thought about what happened during Mike II's month of seclusion. Then in 1996, Jack Gilmore took a creative writing class. Gilmore had been the athletic department's business manager in 1956, and because of his position, he was privy to a few secrets concerning Mike II.

Gilmore wrote an essay giving a new account of the early days of Mike II's reign. This essay was published in the magazine section of the September 1, 1996, issue of *The Advocate*. It was called "The Year of the Tiger, a Secret Revealed," and exposed the fact that Mike II did actually die on a day in mid-October, 1956, only three weeks after his tenure as mascot began. Interestingly, according to the Chinese zodiac 1956 was not the Year of the Tiger, but the Year of the Monkey. The Year of the Monkey is described as follows: clever and skillful to the point of genius, practical and given to detail, you generally have a low opinion of others. Your best relationships are with the Dragon, Rat and Ram and not so good with the Tiger.

Jack Gilmore joined the LSU community in April of 1955. He, along with athletic director Jim Corbett and football coach Paul Dietzel, was hired to help rejuvenate a failing football program. The trio was greeted with enthusiasm and high hopes by the LSU faithful. Those hopes did not fade even after the 1955 season turned into a disappointment; after all, even the best head coach needs a season to "rebuild." The 1956 season was expected to be a great success, but by October LSU had a losing record, and the previous year's enthusiasm was soon replaced by exasperation with the new arrivals.

Into this not-quite-friendly atmosphere came what must have seemed like a disaster. Early one mid-October morning the campus security chief, Dick Anderson, discovered the young Mike II sprawled out motionless on the floor of his cage. He called Jim Corbett, who in turn called Jack Gilmore. The three men entered the cage, confirmed that Mike II was dead, and then sat down to discuss their options. It was easy for the men closely aquatinted with athletic department public relations to imagine how the press would react to the death of LSU's brand-new mascot.

Jim Corbett anticipated how the newspaper stories would likely read: "The football team is so bad that even the Tiger could not bear the shame; he took the easy way out." With public relations in mind, the three men made a decision to cover up the mascot's death.

Corbett issued a press release saying that Mike II was ill and would be kept in seclusion until his health improved; later he issued another release saying that the mascot had been moved to the New Orleans Zoo for treatment by the zoo's experts. Jack Gilmore made calls to the Seattle and New Orleans Zoos, arranging to purchase a new cub from Seattle and have it delivered to Audubon Zoo. Mike II was buried somewhere on the batten side of Mississippi River levee, and his replacement was transferred from Audubon Zoo to LSU, placed into the cage, and proclaimed completely recovered.

The cause of the original Mike II's death will probably never be known, but records from Audubon Zoo shed a little light on the mystery. Mike II was part of a litter of three cubs born at Audubon Zoo, which consisted of two males and a female. Audubon has records of the routine health evaluations done on each of the cubs as well as copies of the correspondence between LSU and Audubon officials negotiating the purchase of one of the males to serve as LSU's mascot. These records show that the female cub of the litter died about one month before the males did. Both males died within a week of each other. Apparently Mike II really was brought to Audubon to be examined by the experts, as Corbett's press release stated. The examination, however, was an autopsy, not a precursor to medical treatment. In the medical and postmortem records from Audubon, the two male cubs were referred to as "male cub 1" and "male cub 2", so we have no evidence as to which of these was Mike. One cub presumably died from heart failure. The other died from pneumonia. The examining vet at the zoo also noted that this cub had two fractured ribs, one on each side.

It was not long after the second Mike II was installed that he started having problems of his own. In October of 1957, approximately ten months after he made his secret arrival on campus, he fractured his leg. Then, seven months after his first injury, he was sent to Audubon Zoo for treatment of multiple fractures of the leg; he died there on May 15, 1958, of pneumonia.

The LSU community was appropriately sad for the occasion of Mike II's death, but the outpouring of grief was not as poignant as it had been for Mike I. "We just didn't have as much time to get attached," said one student. An editorial in the *Reveille* entitled "Let's Not Forget" urged students to raise money for preserving Mike II. "We should have him stuffed, just as Mike I was stuffed...after all, it would be nice to have two tigers to put in the new Student Union building, when it is completed, and to start a collection." This idea did not come to pass, as Mike II was not sent to a taxidermist. Once again, the LSU community set its sights on securing a new mascot.

Mike III

On May 21, 1958, the fundraiser to buy Mike III began. Students and alumni, reminded that the student body had paid for Mike I and Mike II, were asked to contribute money for the new mascot via a campaign nicknamed "Feed the Kitty." At one point, the mascot's traveling cage was parked outside the Gym Armory on LSU campus. Students were able to place donations into a basket inside the cage. Alumni were encouraged to mail donations to "Mike III Fund c/o Student Council, Louisiana State University." Perhaps the exodus of students for summer break contributed to the lackluster success of the fundraising drive. In the end, the Athletic Department had to advance the Student Government Association $500 of the $950 purchase price.

The tiger was bought from the Seattle Zoo, the same place that supplied the second Mike II. The new tiger was born on Nov. 28, 1957 and arrived at the LSU campus on Aug. 29, 1958. He was flown from Seattle to Chicago, and from there to New Orleans, a trip that cost $150. Flying Tiger Airlines provided the travel for the first leg of little Mike's journey. This piece of trivia became a part of LSU lore–so, too, did the fact that the LSU football Tigers had an undefeated season, the first in 50 years, and won the national championship during Mike III's first season as mascot.

Mike III is widely known as the most successful mascot to date. If the criterion for success is the record of the football team, Mike III is indeed worthy of such accolades. However, the arrival of Mike III did not appear to attract the student-driven pandemonium of prior mascots, and no academic holiday was granted for the occasion.

1958 was an eventful year for Mike as well as for LSU. The tiger made the trip to the 1958 Sugar Bowl where he watched his football counterparts win the game and the national championship. But in October of 1958, shortly before the homecoming game with Florida and five months after his introduction into the cage, Mike III broke both his hind legs. He was the second, and possibly the third tiger to be seriously injured in two years. This injury precipitated the removal of a screen that had been placed over the bars of the cage shortly after Mike I died. After the screen was removed, the injuries stopped. The cubs had been observed climbing to the roof of the enclosure, which was possible to do with the mesh barrier. Some speculated that falls associated with this climbing were responsible for the injuries to the cubs. This conjecture was not proven and probably will forever remain a mystery.

In terms of personality, Mike III was known as a vicious, unhappy tiger that did not like people. Dr. Sheldon Bivin, the veterinarian in charge of the mascot, described Mike III as crotchety and thought it was probably due to the fact that he had a degenerative bone condition and was in constant pain.

"He was always an angry, suspicious animal. He fussed and growled every time we came near him. His instinct was to fight for life," Bivin said.

Mike III was almost euthanized in the early 1970s due to the degenerative bone condition and severe arthritis, but decision-makers relented, and Mike lived out his years in the cage before dying of complications from old age.

In 1974, Georgia Tucker Smith wrote a children's book entitled *Mike the Tiger Enrolls at LSU.* This is the only known book written on Mike the Tiger, and it recounts the story of Mike I from birth to death. However, the story includes noteworthy events from the lives of Mike II, Mike III and the first Mike IV, who was the only mascot to be acquired before the death of his predecessor.

During the reign of Mike III, LSU acquired two additional mascots. The first one made his debut at the 1959 season opener against Rice University. A stadium full of shocked football fans watched as the tiger's traveling cage gates were opened and its occupant jumped out. Fans cheered as they realized that the tiger was not Mike III, but a person dressed in a tiger suit. This mascot still graces LSU sporting events today and is a character unto himself.

The second new mascot was an actual tiger cub. On Jan. 1, 1971, LSU played in the Orange Bowl in Miami. One of the Orange Bowl organizers owned a six-month-old 65-pound tiger cub appropriately named Cajun. The cub was turned loose during the LSU practice the day before the Orange bowl. He endeared himself to the football team by playfully biting head coach Charles McClendon and tearing up a football jersey. His frisky antics on the sidelines during the Orange Bowl captured the hearts of LSU fans on the nationally televised game.

Several members of the LSU Board of Supervisors pooled their money and purchased the cub for $900. James T. Staples, chairman of the Board of Supervisors, was quoted on Jan. 9, 1971, as saying that the tiger belonged to LSU and had been renamed Mike IV. The tiger was flown from Miami to New Orleans, where he spent the night with football player Mark Lumpkin and his wife. A New Orleans veterinarian thoroughly checked the young cub and proclaimed him to be in excellent condition. However, a quandary ensued when the cub was moved from New Orleans to Baton Rouge, because there was no place to put him. Mike IV could not be moved into Mike III's cage. In Sheldon Bivin's words, "Mike would have torn him to pieces!" There were no facilities available at the Baton Rouge Zoo for housing the young cub. Staples thought that perhaps he could keep the young tiger at his house, but according to his friend and rescuer Marvin Allain, his wife told him, "Either you get that tiger out, or you're both out!" At this point, the desperate Staples found solace in Allain, who agreed to care for Mike IV until alternative facilities could be arranged. Allain was experienced in working with exotic animals, as he lived with two pet lions.

The public was kept abreast of the early events of the new mascot's life. On Feb. 4, 1971, the tiger paid a visit to the *Baton Rouge Morning Advocate*, where he was fed a stick of candy and relaxed on the publisher's couch. There were also pictures of Cajun/Mike IV in the 1971 issue of *Gumbo*.

Cajun lived with Marvin Allain for about a year. During this time, Allain called the cat "Mike" and treated him as a pet. "I was happy to help out Jake [Staples]," Allain said in an interview. "I was really lucky to share my life with Mike. He was a sweetheart, and there was not a mean bone in his body. I treated him, and all my wild animals, the way I wanted to be treated. As long as you do that and are consistent, the animals are great. I have never been bitten or hurt by any wild animal. Mike was sixteen to seventeen inches long when I got him, and he was full length by the time he left. He slept in bed with me every night, and I never had to put him in a cage. He just lived in the house and in my fenced-in backyard.

"Jake and his brother owned and operated Bob and Jake's, a restaurant which was the 'place to be' in Baton Rouge. Two or three times a week, Jake called me and told me to come over and to bring Mike. I'd walk the tiger around the restaurant on a leash; he was tame and the diners really loved the entertainment. Then Jake fed him a ribeye steak.

"This was our routine for about a year, but while I had Mike, the Baton Rouge Zoo was building a temporary facility to house him. When they completed it, I had to take Mike to the zoo. I was attached to him, so it was really hard to give him up. In fact, I was so depressed that I went out and bought a cougar.

"I visited Mike frequently while he was in the Baton Rouge Zoo. He was kept in a small enclosure, and when I came in, the keepers let me get in there with him. After the zoo closed and the public wasn't around, I was allowed to take him out of confinement and walk him around. About nine months after he entered the zoo, I moved from Baton Rouge and couldn't visit him anymore."

Although Mike IV/Cajun was intended as the successor to Mike III, he never attained that position. Allain heard that something happened to Mike's leg or paw, and that he never became mascot as a result of the injury. The one published reference regarding the fate of the tiger reported that he developed a paw deformity, was thus deemed inappropriate as mascot material, and was subsequently sold to a small zoo. Other sources (who asked not to be identified) report that the tiger died at the Baton Rouge Zoo. We have been unable to corroborate either claim with documentable evidence.

During the time that Mike IV was living with Marvin Allain, Mike III still acted as the official mascot for LSU but slowly succumbed to the illnesses of old age. As Mike aged, those concerned with the mascot and his living conditions mounted a concerted effort to address this issue. One *Advocate* reader stated in a letter to the editor, "I have a difficult time believing that Mike III felt any affection for the LSU student body since he was jailed in that absurdly small cage for these 18 years and systematically abused in the LSU stadium every fall."

Some students reportedly felt it was cruel to enclose the 450-500 pound mascot in a 600-square-foot cage. Sentiments of this sort may have been on the rise as a result of the actions of the World Wildlife Fund (WWF) and other organizations. In 1972, the WWF reported that only 2,000 Bengal tigers were left alive in the world; they estimated that unless steps were taken to prevent their extinction, all Bengal tigers would vanish by 1982. The passage of the Endangered Species Act in 1973 may also have contributed to the public's growing concern for Mike's well-being. All subspecies of tigers were placed on the endangered species list at this time, and the issue of Mike's welfare became, and still is, the subject of public debate.

It was in this spirit that a campaign for a new cage for the mascot was initiated in November of 1975. Student organizers hoped to raise $40,000 for an enlarged cage with a natural habitat. Their main concerns were that Mike had inadequate space for exercise and that he had a completely unnatural habitat in which to live. He was still living in the cage built in 1937, and many thought the cage was outdated and inadequate. The students expected that it would take several years to raise the needed funds.

This was not the first time students had tried to improve Mike's living conditions. Lloyd Dore, an LSU law student, said that in 1972 the student government had tried to begin a similar fundraiser, but "got a lot of flak from the athletic department."

Mike III, however, was not to benefit from these efforts. In early August of 1976, Mike was hospitalized at the LSU veterinary medical school. The degenerative bone condition he had been battling for years rendered him unable to walk or eat, as his jaw was set in a permanently shut position. A debate on euthanizing the ailing mascot raged among the members of the LSU community; however, Mike III died before this issue was resolved. He passed away on the night of August 11, 1976. Coincidentally, lockjaw brought the demise of Eddie the Educated Vegetable Man in 1946, and thirty years later, Mike III fell victim to the same affliction.

Some suggested that the Louisiana weather contributed to Mike's demise. A newspaper article from August 22, 1976, reported, "Although he hesitated before he said it, Dr. Bivin believes the summer heat in Mike III's cage was responsible for much of his deterioration. In the hottest months, Mike III's appetite was poor." Air-conditioning was installed in the enclosed part of the cage before Mike IV arrived on August 31, 1976.

Officials sought to preserve Mike III as they had Mike I; however, the body had decomposed by the time it reached the taxidermists. The taxidermists were able to salvage Mike's head, which they mounted on a large wooden plaque. Mike III's head adorned the walls of Gold Star Trophies in Baton Rouge for many years. It is now in a private home.

With Mike III's death, the question arose of whether or not another mascot should be obtained. Gilmore commented, "It was never seriously considered that we not get another mascot. There was general consensus of opinion that the people wanted a mascot...after all, LSU has had a mascot for 40 years." Despite opinions to the contrary, LSU had a new tiger within a month.

The 1973 Endangered Species Act made the buying and selling of tigers for commercial gain illegal. Consequently, a tiger had to be donated to the university. Mike III's successor was a gift from Busch Gardens of Tampa, Florida. He was born there on May 15, 1973, on the 15th anniversary of the second Mike II's death.

Mike IV

Mike IV came to LSU on Aug. 29, 1976, to begin service as mascot exactly 18 years after Mike III arrived. This Mike was the oldest tiger to begin service as mascot. At 27 months of age, he already weighed 450 pounds and was full-grown. He was given the name Mike IV but was in reality the second Mike IV and the sixth tiger LSU owned. Once again, while there was excitement on behalf of the new mascot, no student holiday was declared, and no pandemonium ensued.

The cage expansion campaign continued after the new tiger's arrival. In May of 1981, LSU awarded a contract for

Mike IV. Courtesy of LSU, University Relations.

the construction of the cage, in the amount of $96,900, to Riverside of Louisiana. On June 2, Mike was moved from Baton Rouge to a temporary residence at a zoo in Little Rock, Arkansas. The deadline for completion of the construction was the beginning of football season the following September.

Bivin was not impressed with the completed cage, even though it sported a pool and waterfall, a climbing platform, rock work, a grassy area, and almost 2000 square feet of living area, up from the original 600.

"That cage wound up costing three times as much as it was supposed to and was one-third the size it was supposed to be," he said. Although Bivin wished he and the university had been more vigilant with respect to the cage-building contract, the new $175,000 cage was a definite improvement over the original.

Mike IV was vicious and ferocious, as Mike III had been. However, while Mike III's surliness was attributed to physical pain, Mike IV's mood was not. "Mike IV was mean-spirited and aggressive," reported Bivin.

This tiger has had perhaps the most action-packed life of any of the mascots. Soon after he was installed in his new cage, Mike IV accomplished the tiger stunt to end all tiger stunts. He escaped. On the night of Nov. 28, 1981, Mike IV somehow got out of his cage. Officials assume that a prankster aided his escape, but no one knows for sure. A privileged few people were thrown into a wild panic that night, as they found themselves confronted with the unenviable task of returning the 500-pound adult male tiger to its rightful place. An article from a 1995 edition of the *Advocate* looked back on the evening with nostalgia and recounted the following events:

Officer Pam Anderson, who had the misfortune to be working the LSU police station communications desk that night, received news of the escape from a breathless man who ran into her office at approximately 11:30 p.m., announced his discovery, and departed as quickly as he'd come. She was shocked when the officer she radioed confirmed the news. "That's a ten-four. He's out."

The officer had driven up to Mike, who was standing in the middle of North Stadium Drive. He reported that the tiger's head was as high as the police cruiser's mirror. Undaunted by the company, Mike proceeded to knock down two pine trees before heading toward the cage and Bernie Moore Track Stadium.

Bivin, who had the flu, was roused from bed to deal with the situation. The plan of action in a tiger escape is to return the animal to his cage unharmed. This will happen if the animal is herded back into the cage, returns of his own volition, or is tranquilized and physically returned by his captors. But if human life is in immediate danger, the animal is killed. Fortunately for the LSU community, danger to people was not imminent by virtue of the late hour and Thanksgiving break, which had cleared the campus of most human occupants.

Bivin and police officers herded Mike into Bernie Moore Track Stadium, where Bivin prepared to tranquilize the tiger. Bivin hit Mike with the first dart he fired, and the tiger bolted about thirty yards down the field as a result, fortunately not in Bivin's direction. The second hit brought Mike walking drunkenly toward Bivin. The third shot knocked him out, and six men secured Mike with ropes and brought him back to his cage in the back of a pickup truck. "You won't find this in any newspaper," confided Bivin, "but when I shot that last dart, he was charging me. I had my shotgun with me; thank God I didn't have to use it." Mike was a little woozy from the tranquilizer but was back to normal in 36 hours.

In addition to being the first and only LSU mascot to escape, Mike IV was also the first LSU mascot to be seen on the silver screen. In February 1988, the movie *Everybody's All-American*, was filmed in Baton Rouge. The movie was about LSU football player Gavin Grey, nicknamed "Grey Ghost." Mike IV was one of the stars of this movie, along with Dennis Quaid and Jessica Lange. Mike took part in a parade that wound its way down Fourth Street toward the state capitol and was also pictured in his traveling cage inside Tiger Stadium.

Mike was a key player in a scene of international intrigue. In April 1988, a man named Moacyr Cezar, oddly enough nicknamed "el Gato," or "the Cat," locked himself into one of the portions of Mike's cage. He had been in the United States for approximately two years working as a proctor in the athletes' dorm in exchange for room and board.

His visa did not allow him to work for money, so he had had no income during the time he spent in the USA. One afternoon, the frustration of his financial situation and the fact that his visa would soon expire led him to take desperate measures.

He grabbed the keys to the cage from Mike's keeper, announced that he had a gun and a bomb, and locked himself into the smaller half of Mike's cage in an act of protest. Fortunately, Mike was secured in the adjoining part of the cage. Cezar demanded to see LSU basketball coach Dale Brown, who was in Florida at the time. Cezar explained later his thought that Brown, who had been trying to help Cezar find work on campus, could offer more assistance than he had been giving.

Police enlisted the help of basketball standout Jose Vargas, with whom Cezar had formed a relationship, and Reverend Ramon Vega, who both spoke Cezar's native Portuguese, to defuse the situation. After five hours of negotiating, the two men persuaded Cezar to leave the cage. It was then found that he was carrying only a toy gun. Mr. Cezar apologized to the LSU community for his actions and shortly thereafter returned to his native Brazil, where he had been a star basketball player.

Also in April 1988, a Baton Rouge couple, Rock and Ramelle Rockhold, donated a female Bengal tiger cub named Reena to LSU. They had been given the cub as a gift and decided that LSU would be a good home for her when she grew to adulthood. The couple reached an agreement with LSU that allowed the Rockholds to keep the cat until it was sexually mature, at about three years of age.

University officials foresaw a number of possibilities concerning the use of the cub. They hoped that she might become the future mother of Mike V and considered using her as an additional mascot. Mike Archer, the head football coach, did a commercial with the little cub.

Unfortunately for Reena, the Rockholds' neighbors complained to East Baton Rouge Parish Animal Control about having a pet tiger in the neighborhood, and the Rockholds were subsequently refused a permit to keep her. She had to be moved to the Baton Rouge Zoo and experienced quite a change from the hand feeding and pampering she was used to. LSU's involvement with the tiger apparently ended here, and Reena lives at the Baton Rouge Zoo today.

The next big event in Mike IV's life was the arrival of Mike V. In November 1989, Bivin decided to make a departure from tradition and retire Mike IV before the cat became old and ill. When Mike III died, Bivin had been at the center of a storm of anger and grief from Tiger fans. To avoid this type of outcry, LSU instituted a policy of retiring the mascots at 15 years of age.

Mike IV was transferred from the tiger cage at LSU to the Baton Rouge Zoo in late April of 1990. Published reasons for this course of action were the stress Mike incurred from constant exhibition and the pinched nerves in his back. Anonymous sources say that Mike IV had difficulty adjusting to his new surroundings, possibly because there were other tigers in his cage. Mike IV remained at the Baton Rouge Zoo until March 3, 1995, when he was euthanized because of seriously declining health.

There was no discussion as to whether or not LSU should obtain another mascot when Mike IV died, as there had been at the end of Mike III's reign. A new mascot was already in place and had been for five years.

Mike V

Once the decision was made to retire Mike IV, the University began a search for his successor. LSU obtained a cub and named him Mike V, but exams revealed he had incurable cataracts. He was euthanized because he would never be able to see properly. Bivin continued his search and located a second cub, the current Mike V.

Bivin procured the tiger from a couple in Moulton, Alabama, who ran a small zoological park. This couple, the Atchisons, owned several lions, tigers, bears and other exotic animals. Mike V was born on October 5, 1989, to tigers owned by the Atchisons.

Mike V's original name was Stevie, and there were two other cubs in his litter, both males. One of those tigers went to Hollywood and appeared in a movie about Mother Teresa. The other went to the Earl Flynn Ranch in Aspen, Colorado; he is exhib-

Mike V. Courtesy of LSU, University Relations.

ited at an area casino. Mike V has another full brother who serves as the mascot for the University of Memphis and is named TOM II. Mike's brother was born on July 17, 1991 in a different litter but to the same parents. TOM II has been with the University of Memphis since November 16, 1991, and at this time, is the only other live tiger university mascot in the nation. He is currently housed in a 3,500-square-foot all-natural facility at St. Nick's Farm in Memphis. This facility was built for TOM in 1992 and cost $310,000.

On February 13, 1990, ten-week-old Stevie paid a visit to Mike IV, who was still serving as LSU's official mascot. Bivin greeted the public with the 69-pound cub (secured on a leash) and introduced him to the media. Mike V growled into a television camera before being led to the bars of the cage housing the current mascot. Mike IV came down from his perch above the waterfall in the cage to greet Mike V. The tigers touched noses through the bars of the cage; however, Mike IV quickly lost interest in the cub and walked away after emitting a noise somewhere between a cough and a roar.

"At least he appears to recognize him as one of his own species," Bivin said of Mike IV. The noise Mike IV made could very well have been an example of prustening. Prustening is a German word, literally meaning "to blow air through one's teeth." It is a tiger's greeting. Perhaps in his own tiger way, Mike IV passed the mascot torch on to Mike V.

After the tigers met, Bivin introduced the cub to the LSU students assembled for the event. Mike V rolled over to have his belly scratched, and the students responded by ruffling his ears and petting him. To involve the public in the new cub's arrival, LSU invited everyone interested to have their picture taken with him. The cub was small enough to pose no significant danger to the public.

Mike V was formally introduced to LSU fans at a February 21, 1990, basketball game against Alabama. He officially began his reign as the tiger mascot on April 30, 1990, when he moved into the tiger cage vacated by Mike IV.

Mike V's life has been relatively uneventful to this point, as he has not experienced kidnappings or escapes as some of the former mascots. The vet school provides his daily care; two veterinary students feed Mike, clean the cage, and check him daily on an alternating weekly schedule. The students are elected for two-year terms that run during their third and fourth years of veterinary training. LSU associate professor Dr. David Baker is the veterinarian in charge of Mike V.

Mike enjoys watching people walk along North Stadium drive; sometimes you will find him sleeping on his back with his paws in the air. Mike V is widely regarded as the mascot with the best disposition of all the tigers LSU has used. Mike is usually more active at night and during colder weather. Mike V also has his little quirks, as relayed by former keeper Shane Parker.

"After we've cleaned out his cage, if one of us moves his beer keg [a toy] from the spot it was in when we first came in, the first thing Mike will do when we let him back out into the cage is to move it. It's like a game he plays; he has to have the last paw on his beer keg. Also, if you hose off any part of his cage, he'll spray it to make it his territory again. Once in awhile he'll have a reaction to a person coming up to see him, and he will spray at that person. He can hit people with spray, even through the cage bars and chain link fence."

One alumnus said, "The first year Mike was in the cage, I used to come down here in my rollerblades or on my bike, and I'd ride around the perimeter of the cage. Mike would chase me around the perimeter; he was really excited about doing this."

Mike V still participates in the long-standing tradition of riding around Tiger Stadium before home football games. He is occasionally brought to the Pete Maravich Assembly Center for home basketball games and to Alex Box Stadium for baseball games. In 1997, a brand new traveling cage was built to replace the 27-year-old cage in use at the time.

On May 13, 1997, veterinary dental specialist Ben Colmery performed root canal surgery on Mike's lower right canine tooth at LSU's School of Veterinary Medicine. Mike had broken his tooth, probably from a fall in his cage a few weeks prior to the operation. The surgery was successful, and Mike was returned to the cage after an overnight observational stay at the vet school. Mike's toothache did not go unnoticed by UGA, the University of Georgia bulldog mascot, who sent Mike a get-well card. UGA was returning the favor; Mike sent him similar sentiments in 1996 for a minor illness, which was apparently not the first of its kind. John Berendt described an earlier exchange in which Mike the Tiger sent UGA IV a get-well card for knee surgery in his nonfiction bestseller, *Midnight in the Garden of Good and Evil.*

On April 19, 2000, officials announced their intention to build a new habitat for Mike the Tiger. This enclosure will be substantially larger than the current cage and will contain a natural, enriched environment. Fundraising and design activities are currently underway.

The average life span of a tiger in captivity at the present time is 18 years, though captive tigers can live to be 25. If Mike V reaches the average, he will be with us for a long time to come.

Andrea Albright and Marybeth Lima want to acknowledge Lakiesha Claude, Nicholas Coleman, and Kim Hill for assisting with data collection. They also gratefully acknowledge the many people who shared research material and anecdotes, including Marvin Allain, Sheldon Bivin, Portia Lepage Conrad, the late Jack Fiser, the late Dee Dee Fulmer-Gilbert, and Eddie Laborde.

Lima can be reached at: Department of Biological and Agricultural Engineering, Room 149 E.B. Doran Building, LSU, Baton Rouge, LA 70803-4505.

CHAPTER 8

Herb Vincent: SID Insider

Herb Vincent was the sports information di rector at LSU for 12 years, from 1988- 2000. He worked with four head football coaches, starting with Mike Archer. To say that Vincent saw some things would be an understatement. His side of the hirings and firings are something else.

Archer's End

"The worst Archer story was when I had to go out and tell him that Channel 2 was report- ing the story that he was going to get fired at the end of the year. And his reaction to it shocked me," Vincent said.

"I was just telling him so he could tell the players, 'Look, you're going back to the dorm, you're gonna see this story, don't pay any attention to it'. That wasn't the reaction he had.

"I tell him this, and I leave to go back to the office to watch the story on television. I watch it and I go back out to practice because I know all heck is going to break loose. And all the players are coming off the field and saying, 'Bad scene, man, bad scene. Coach Archer's crying. He's all upset.'

"So I get on the bus, and he's the only one sitting there, and he's crying. 'Coach, there's nothing to the story. I've talked to Joe. I was just telling you so you'd know.' And he's all upset because he believes it.

"It turns out several people had told him before that day he'd better watch out, they're already getting ready to fire you. So when it was on TV I guess it made it true to him. And that's why he broke down about it.

"We went back to the office, and Joe Dean was talking to a booster club in Lake Charles. I told him everything that happened. He told me to get Coach Archer and he'd come back to meet him.

"Joe and Mike sat and talked. Joe told him there was nothing to the story and that that decision had not been made. He says, 'As a matter of fact, I talked to [chancellor] Bud Davis this morning and he's insistent on you staying for another year.' And Joe had told me that earlier in the day, even before the Channel 2 story had come out. And Archer said, 'I can't stay here now, not under these circumstances. I won't be able to recruit now.'

"It got loud between the two of them. He wasn't angry, just upset. I don't know what happened between that time and the next morning. I was telling him not to make a decision when he was very emotional. And then the next morning he said he couldn't stay. But he made it clear to me that in the release he didn't want to say that he resigned and he didn't want it to say he was fired. 'So what you do you want me to say?'

"If you go back and read the release, it said he stepped down as head coach, or something like that. But he finished out the season."

Herb Vincent. Courtesy of LSU Sports Information.

Bring Back the Magic

Gerry DiNardo wowed LSU fans when he got the job, touring the state and taking it by storm with his charismatic speeches.

"When the *Advocate* ran the headline 'Bring Back the Magic,' it was a perfect name for the tour," Vincent recalled. "The reason I wanted to do that was here was a guy from Vanderbilt and Notre Dame, LSU's big rival. He wasn't a popular choice and obviously wasn't a big-name college football coach. But once you heard him speak, people liked him. So I felt like the more people we could put him in front of, the better.

"He was very cooperative, and so we brought him around the whole state. The key to the 'Bring Back the Magic' tour was [that] you had to see him in person to understand what he was all about."

Good Preparation

"I did with Gerry what I did with every other coach: I gave him all the press clippings from all the football coaches from their first day at LSU so he'd get an idea of what the questions would be. He really got into that. I started asking him questions and quizzing him. He said, 'Give me questions, give me questions!' So we'd have a practice press conference. And he was always prepared. On Tuesdays before his weekly luncheon we'd do that, and it was the ideal relationship for an SID and a football coach."

DiNardo's Demise and Clean Toilets

"The hardest thing was that morning. I woke up and Joe called me at home and said I needed to come meet him and then go meet the chancellor in his office. This was right after the Houston game.

"So I get there and he says, 'It's over.' So we go meet the chancellor, Mark Emmert, and we talked about what was going to happen that day. And they asked how Gerry was going to react. And I really didn't know. I didn't know if he wanted to coach, not coach, but we talked about them meeting with Gerry and then having a press conference.

"I had to write a statement for Joe, I had to write a statement for the chancellor, and I had to write a press release and get all that done that morning. The worst part of it was Gerry would call me–I don't know how many times a day–just to say, 'What's going on? What's happenin'?' And I didn't want to get that call that morning.

"That was one of the things we had going on. We would never lie to each other. But we could always tell when we didn't want to say something to each other. So I didn't want to get that call from him. So I told Joe I was going home to write all that stuff.

"I got everything written, but I still had time for the press conference. I knew what time Joe was going to talk to Gerry, and I didn't want to go back to school and get that call.

"So I just hung out at my house and I cleaned the toilets...that was a good thing that came out of that morning.

"In the meantime, [Gerry] was trying to reach me. He couldn't find me and called [his wife] Terry and told her,

'Something's up. I can't find Herb, and I can always find Herb.'"

The Hiring of Nick Saban

"The way I knew a candidate was coming to the forefront for the search committee people [was that] Joe would call me and say, 'Get me all the information you can on so-and-so.' He called me on Thanksgiving morning and asked if I had a Michigan State media guide and that he needed as much information on Nick Saban as I could get him.

"That was the first time his name had come up. Joe said, 'You can't tell anybody. You can't let anybody see you copy that stuff and drop it off at my house.' So I went to the office and copied all the stuff I could find on Nick Saban and dropped it at his house and didn't say a word to anybody until they told me they were going to have a press conference [the following Tuesday].

"I had no idea it was going to happen that fast. Joe said, 'I think it's going to happen today.' And I said, 'Really? Well, who's it going to be?' Usually by then, when we're going to have a press conference, the SID knows who it will be.

"Joe says, 'It's going to be Nick Saban, and we're paying him 1.2...million...dollars.' He says it like that. My jaw must have dropped."

The News Conference

"**I** gave him the same kind of list of questions [that I gave DiNardo]. It was a brief thing. With DiNardo, I had the whole night before. We announced him by sending out a press release saying that Gerry DiNardo was going to be announced as head coach tomorrow. With Saban it was boom-boom-boom-boom."

Saban had barely slept from the time he left East Lansing until he arrived in Baton Rouge early in the morning.

"I could tell how tired and worn out and shocked he was by the whole thing. He did his press conference and we took him back into the office and he was just sitting there [quiet and stone-faced]. Because things happened so fast."

After that, Saban went out for a more informal question-and-answer session with the media.

"It was just the usual routine for a new LSU football coach. We got it down to a routine after a while."

CHAPTER 9

A Converted Tiger, A Trainer's Tales and LeBlanc's Memories

Jim Collier became something he never thought he would: An LSU Tiger.

Jim Collier stayed in his home state and played at Arkansas from 1959-61. He jokes today that he was the guy who made coach Frank Broyles famous. But he did have a heck of a career, one that continued in the NFL before he ended up in Baton Rouge as a coach on Charles McClendon's staff from 1965-79.

In the 1962 NFL title game, only two touchdowns were scored, and both came from players with LSU ties. The Packers, who won the game, got their touchdown from Tigers great Jimmy Taylor. The Giants' TD came from Jim Collier, who recovered a blocked punt in the end zone.

Collier, a receiver, didn't see a lot of playing time, because he was listed behind Frank Gifford, Del Shofner and

Jim Collier. Courtesy of LSU, University Relations.

Joe Walton in New York. "I didn't run fast enough to play in the pros," he admitted.

But he may be the winningest assistant coach in LSU history, considering that during his tenure, the Tigers' record was 113-52-5.

Great Receivers

C ollier coached receivers at LSU. "The ones who dropped the passes," he joked.

The first great receiver he coached didn't have that problem. It was Doug Moreau (LSU 1963-65), now the East Baton Rouge district attorney. Another favorite was Andy Hamilton (LSU 1969-71).

"He was Bert Jones's cousin. Their mommas were sisters. I don't know if people know that. He averaged over 20 yards a catch and caught three touchdown passes against Notre Dame.

"And Carlos Carson (LSU 1977-79) once caught six consecutive passes for six consecutive touchdowns. He caught five passes for touchdowns against Rice when we beat 'em 77-0 [in 1977], and the following week we played Florida and the first pass he caught was a touchdown [in a 36-14 victory]."

Beating his Alma Mater

C ollier never played against LSU while he was at Arkansas, but his first season at LSU, the Tigers went to the Cotton Bowl and played the Razorbacks.

"We would never tell the players this, because we never thought we would lose the game. But as coaches we knew that Arkansas had such great talent and all that. They had a 22-game winning streak. We would look at those films and it was really something. We'd say, 'How are we going to beat these guys?' It comes from the heart."

LSU had plenty of heart on Jan. 1, 1966, beating Arkansas 14-7.

Signing Lew

The recruiting game can get nasty, especially if it involves your alma mater, as Collier will attest.

"I signed a kid named Lew Sibley, who started for us as a freshman," Collier recalled of Lewellyn Sibley of Longview, Tx. (LSU 197-77), an All-SEC defensive end in 1976.

"I was recruiting him and all, but his coach called down here and said he was going to sign with Arkansas. So I told Coach McClendon, 'I'll get him.' So I went back over there.

"I sat down with Lew and I asked him, 'When you get through with Arkansas, are you going to raise chickens or are you going to raise turkeys? Because that's all they've got in Arkansas.'

Lew Sibley. Courtesy of LSU Sports Information.

"Well, he got mad and he started out to the yard and I grabbed him by the shoulder. And he turned around and he knocked me down. He hit me right across the chest and knocked me down.

"To make a long story short, on the day of the signing, I went upstairs to where they lived in an apartment complex. I got there early in the morning. Signing didn't start until 8 o'clock. I got there in time to see them throw the newspaper. Finally, here came the coach from Arkansas."

The Arkansas coach, whose name Collier could not recall, told him everything looked good for Sibley to sign with the Razorbacks.

"Anyway, we go upstairs and knock on the door and shoot the bull for about 10 minutes. And Lew finally says to the Arkansas coach, 'Coach, I appreciate everything you've done, but I'm going to LSU.' And the Arkansas coach went to his knees. He was begging. Begging!

"I said to Lew, 'The only way you're going to get him to quit begging and crying is to sign this,' and I handed him the letter of intent. And the coach from Arkansas left!"

Collier laughed heartily.

"He got fired at Arkansas after I signed Sibley."

Billy Simmons

B illy Simmons was a student at LSU from 1966-70 and then spent two years in graduate school. During that time, he made more than his share of interesting observations as an LSU trainer.

LSU was 5-0 going into the 1969 Auburn game in Tiger Stadium.

"I noticed from the sideline that Jimmy Gilbert was lined up at starting tailback, and Jimmy Gilbert wasn't the starting tailback. And Andy Hamilton was split out wide to the right closest to the LSU bench," Simmons recalled.

"The quarterback, Mike Hillman, took the snap from center and pitched out to Jimmy Gilbert, and he threw a touchdown pass to Andy Hamilton on the first play from scrimmage.

"Both teams were ranked really high, and Auburn had a future Heisman Trophy winner in Pat Sullivan, but Andy caught the touchdown pass and went into the end zone without anyone touching him."

Simmons recalled what Auburn coach Shug Jordan had to say about that play.

"Shoot, I was the closest guy to him," Jordan said.

LSU won the game 21-20. The next week it suffered its only loss in a 9-1 season, 26-23 to Ole Miss in Jackson, Mississippi.

But incredibly, there was no bowl game in the Tigers' future.

"We had the best-balanced football team we'd ever had at LSU," the late Charles McClendon recalled in 2000.

LSU overpowered Mississippi State 61-6 and Tulane 27-0 to end the regular season, but back then bowl bids were still given through back-room deals.

"Finally I had to call the Cotton Bowl on Sunday night to find out what was going on," McClendon said. "Everybody thought we were going to the Cotton Bowl. They said Notre Dame, this is their first time to go to a bowl game, and we're going to go with Notre Dame.

"So I had to go out to the dormitory and tell my players we weren't going bowling. They came down in their underwear, their pajamas, everything, because it was way before class. And when I told them, there was dead silence.

If silence could be heard, you could have heard it then. When I left, I heard there was a little disturbance in the dormitory, they were so upset. I was upset, too.

"All the other bowl people that Saturday night [after the Tulane game] were coming by and congratulating us, saying 'Coach, we wish you the best in the Cotton Bowl.' But it didn't work out. But maybe that helped out when we played Notre Dame a little bit later."

Sort of. The next year, LSU lost at Notre Dame 3-0 in South Bend. But in 1971, Notre Dame visited Tiger Stadium and was dispatched 28-8.

No Chinstrap

Mike Anderson's chinstrap broke in a freshman game in 1967. He had said that he had seen Billy Cannon play the Ole Miss game without a chinstrap, so Anderson figured he could play without one, too.

"Mike made a tackle, and a guy busted him under his lip," Simmons recalled. "And you could literally pick up his lower lip and look down his mouth into his throat. Dr. Strange took him in and sutured him up. Mike got up off the table and ran back in and got on the sideline, got into the game the next play and played the rest of the game."

Six In a Row

Simmons has another favorite story about Anderson:

"The first Peach Bowl we played Florida State [and

won, 31-27, on December 30, 1968]. They had an All-American wide receiver named Ron Sellers and a quarterback who played in the NFL, too [Bill Cappleman]. It was a cold and rainy night in Atlanta. We played at Georgia Tech's stadium.

"What was funny was that several months ago I had read a story where Coach Mac talked about how Tommy Casanova covered Sellers in that game and did such a good job on him. But he was confused, because Casanova was a freshman that year and freshmen were ineligible. Craig Burns, who went to Baton Rouge High with me, actually covered him. He was a baseball player who played for the St. Louis Cardinals in their minor-league organization.

"Anyway, in that game, Burns intercepted a pass and ran back a punt that helped set up the winning touchdown. But before halftime I went in to start making the drinks before the guys got in. They had the PA system piped into the dressing room, and I remember hearing Mike Anderson made six straight tackles. 'Tackle Anderson. Stop by Anderson.'

"The PA guys ran out of ways to describe it."

Lynn LeBlanc

Lynn LeBlanc came to LSU from tiny Crowley, a town in southwest Louisiana. He played at LSU and later coached the Tigers as a member of Charles McClendon's staff. What's more, he almost single-handedly ruined the greatest moment in LSU history. But you'll have to read on to get the rest of the story.

"It's special. To me, it's the No. 1 thing in athletics, LSU football," LeBlanc said.

In the 1955-56 school year, LeBlanc was part of a huge duo from Crowley. He was about 6'2" and 170 pounds, while teammate Dan Underwood was 6'4" and 235. They were being recruited by LSU's Pop Strange, but Southwestern Louisiana Institute (later the University of Southwestern Louisiana and now Louisiana-Lafayette) wasn't giving up on LeBlanc.

"I went to Southwestern, and they made me feel like I was a high school All-American, which I wasn't. But I could play basketball at Southwestern and be close to home. They turned my head."

When he got home that day, LeBlanc admitted he was confused.

"And Coach Pop Strange came to the house. And he told me that Danny had signed. 'Look, we're having a great recruiting season this year and we want you to sign with us.' And I said, 'Coach, I don't know, I'm kind of confused.' And he said, 'Look, I'll tell you one thing: We're going to have a good team with you or without you.' And I got to thinking that I could always leave LSU and go to Southwestern, but I couldn't leave Southwestern and go to LSU. So maybe I'd better take this offer."

Imagine what he would have missed out on had he become a Ragin' Cajun instead of a Tiger.

Defense is the Name of the Game

In the championship year of 1958 LeBlanc recalled, "We were playing Florida [10-7], and I intercepted a pass when they were making a drive late in the game. Only pass I intercepted in my life. I was a defensive end. I was an offensive left and defensive right end. And when the end walked off, you were a linebacker. Anyway, they tried a screen pass late in the game, and I made the only interception of my life. But most of the games that year were close. We had several close calls, but to win the national championship you've got to be able to win the close ones.

"And defense was the name of the game. I've told this to people and they don't believe it, but in 1959, we played seven games without a touchdown scored on us, not the White Team, the Go Team or the Bandits. Not a touchdown scored.

"The first touchdown scored on us in 1959 was against Tennessee. [Warren] Rabb threw a pass out in the flat to Johnny Robinson and they intercepted it and ran it back for a touchdown. That was the only touchdown scored against the White unit in the regular season."

As Talented?

S ome argue that the 1959 team was just as talented or perhaps more so than the 1958 squad. LeBlanc didn't think so, because although the '58 team lost just four players, one was a key factor.

"One football player, his name was Tommy Davis. Tommy Davis was our extra-point, field-goal kicker and punter," said LeBlanc, captain of the 1959 team, "and he opted to go pro. He was eligible for 1959, but he ended up with the San Francisco 49ers and set all kinds of kicking records there. See, against Tennessee we missed by a field goal. A couple of them were almost like extra points, and he would have never missed them."

Davis briefly attended LSU but left to serve in the military. He returned from the service to finish at LSU. He died in 1987, the first member of the 1958 LSU title team to pass away.

Running Up the Score

In 1958, LSU carried out one of the 62-0 victories over Tulane. The game was close after two quarters. "We weren't playing too good. But in the second half..." LeBlanc recalled with a smile, as he explained the reason why the score got so lopsided.

"You could only go into a game twice in a quarter. [The officials] took your number. If you went in twice, you weren't eligible to come back again. How stupid a rule was that?"

Against Tulane, LSU had "33 starters," as Paul Dietzel used to say. The games went something like this:

"The White Team starting group would play the first seven and a half minutes," LeBlanc said. "Then, depending on whether we punted or whatever, the Go Team would go in. They'd try to score, but they'd have to punt.

"Well, the Bandits would go in and stop the [opponents]. Then the Go Team would go back in. They had gone in twice, so the Bandits would go back in and the White Team would still have their one time left.

"No telling how good Cannon would have been if he had been able to play a little longer. He played half the game. Nobody played more than half the game."

Which explains why things got out of hand against Tulane.

"[In] the Tulane game in the fourth quarter, the only team left eligible was the White Team," LeBlanc continued. "We ended up playing the last half of the fourth quarter. They claimed we ran up the score on them, but there was no one eligible to go in. I think Tulane fans are still kind of mad about that because we beat them so bad."

Mac Was the Key

LeBlanc explained: "The defense we played in those days, Charlie Mac was the reason we did it so well. He played and coached for Bear Bryant. Mac was tough. We didn't do a lot of things real different, but the things we did, we did real well.

"You could tell by the amount of points we gave up. Bill Terry was the defensive backfield coach, but Mac was the one who was really instrumental to us being so good in those days. He was just tough. He mixed it up with you sometimes. You'd have a circle drill and if it wasn't going right, he'd show you how. And he'd hit you pretty hard, too.

"I was fortunate enough to coach with him for 11 years, and that was a great experience. My ambition as a player was to play at LSU, and after that, when I became a coach, my ambition was to come back to LSU and coach. I didn't want to coach anywhere else. LSU was the only place. Mac was very instrumental in my becoming a good player, and as a coach, I learned a lot from him."

The Undefeated Season

Regarding LSU's 7-0 victory over Clemson in the Jan. 1, 1959, Sugar Bowl, LeBlanc said, "I may have played the worst game of my life.

"It was a close game. [Red] Brodnax fumbled into the end zone and they recovered. It should have been a touchdown. Otherwise we would have won 14-0."

Did he imagine that that would be the last time LSU would go unbeaten and win a national title?

"That was the first time in 50 years we went undefeated. So in 2008 we're going to do it again," LeBlanc said. "It's hard to win a national championship these days. We haven't won that many conference championships, to tell the truth. We've won a few. But I thought we would have won [the national title] again. In fact, we had a couple of chances when I was coaching.

"In 1969, my first year back at LSU, we only lost one ballgame, to Archie Manning and Ole Miss, 26-23. And we had a chance to tie it and go undefeated. We didn't go to a bowl game that year because that was the first year Notre Dame decided to go.

"We were sitting around the office grading films and we were getting phone calls from different bowls, and Mac was turning them down left and right. In fact, somebody called from the Bluebonnet Bowl and Mac recommended Auburn. They ended up playing and got beat bad [36-7].

"Later on that night we got the phone call, and the Cotton Bowl guy told Coach Mac they were going to take Notre Dame. The Sun Bowl still wanted us to come, but when the players came in, they decided not to go. Of course, we went to the Sun Bowl the next year. But we were three points away from an undefeated season!"

Diversity

LeBlanc was on the forefront of helping LSU sign black football players. Among those he got in the fold were Leonard Marshall, Terry Robiske, Greg Bowser, and Lora Hinton, the first black player to sign with LSU.

LeBlanc's Favorite Players

Simply as a fan, LeBlanc said, "Cannon was great, Robinson was great, but Tommy [Casanova], I don't know if he was the greatest, but if he's not, he's in the top three.

"I guess probably the best player I coached, well, John Adams [LSU 1976-79] was good, Lew Sibley [LSU 1974-77] was good, but I think Lyman White (LSU 1977-80) was probably the best I coached. He had the natural ability. He was a good all-around player with speed. Major Thibodeaux [LSU 1977-80] was good, George Atiyeh [LSU 197-80] was good, but if I had to pick one out, as far as being the best athlete, it was Lyman."

The Rest of the Story

By now you may be wondering just how LeBlanc figured into the most famous play in LSU history. Well, he has a different recollection of Billy Cannon's famous punt return than what you've seen replayed every year at Halloween.

"It was raining that night. It was wet. Both teams punted on third down. Heck, they punted on second down a couple of times just to play defense and make the other team play offense to make a mistake.

"Well, I threw [Ole Miss QB] Jake Gibbs for a 10-yard loss on the play before they punted on third down. I'm a right defensive end. If they punt on third down, you don't have an organized punt return. You're still a defensive end, but if they punt, it's an automatic return to the right. Cannon must have been back anyway.

"Well, I was the first one back there. Robinson threw a block. But if you look at the film that they show every year, you can catch a glimpse of it, but I was the first one back there and I threw myself into one guy, and I almost clipped! Wouldn't that have been something, to have clipped on the most famous runback in history? I get up and I'm watching it with the guy I blocked."

Did LeBlanc know he was witnessing what would become the most famous play in LSU history?

"Nah. I was gasping for air."

CHAPTER 10

Even More
Big Hits

Can you name the three former LSU stars in the Pro Football Hall of Fame in Canton, Ohio? The answers and stories about them are at the end of this chapter.

Purple, Gold, White, Whatever

As mentioned earlier in the Gerry DiNardo chapter, the color of the LSU uniforms has been quite a topic of conversation at times, never more so than in the late 1990s, when DiNardo successfully petitioned the SEC to allow the Tigers to wear white jerseys at home.

"You had to get permission before the season started from the team you were playing," LSU equipment manager Jeff Boss said. Of course, LSU upset then No. 1 Florida in Tiger Stadium 28-21 in 1997. Two years later, before the Gators headed back to Baton Rouge, Florida coach Steve Spurrier fired off the following letter to LSU equipment manager Jeff Boss:

Dear Jeff,

Because of the nasty, vulgar treatment our team received from LSU fans during our last visit to Baton Rouge, we have decided that from now on, we will wear the traditional white jersey on the road and dark jersey at home.

Sincerely,
Steve Spurrier
Football Coach

Boss smiled at the memory. "We sat on the letter. We were going to bring it out the week of the game as a psychological ploy."

DiNardo was big on that.

"The most unusual request, of course, was Coach D wanting to be secretive with the purple pants or the time with the white pants and the gold jerseys," Boss said. "And he wanted me to be real secretive when we wore the white helmets."

Anyway, there was always more to the sartorial decisions then met the eye.

Boss remembered, "In the old days, one of the reasons the rule got changed so the visiting team would wear white, well, like when we'd go play Kentucky, we'd bring both sets of jerseys because they wouldn't tell us till the day of the game what color we were wearing."

The Biggest Tiger?

Boss, at LSU since the late 1970s, didn't hesitate when considering the biggest Tiger ever.

"John Tenta, the kid who wrestled, who was a Canadian heavyweight champion, [and] who went to the Olympics."

Just how big was he?

"Oh, God, I don't know," Boss said. "He left here to go be a sumo wrestler. At the time our scale only went to 300 pounds. The trainers had some kind of formula so they could figure out how much you weighed by putting one foot on a brick and another on the scale. So they weighed like half of him. He was like 400 pounds. He was a sumo wrestler for a while and then he came back to the United States as a professional wrestler. He went by 'Earthquake' with this big old tiger tattoo on him.

"He had the biggest head and the biggest body that I've ever had to work with. He wasn't real fast, but if he could catch you he'd bury you."

Tenta, a product of Surry, British Columbia, was later known professionally as "Avalanche" and "Golga." He came to LSU, played football briefly, and when LSU dropped wrestling, Tenta headed to Japan in 1986 to try his hand at sumo wrestling. One of his pro wrestling bios listed him at 6'7", 385 pounds. He was 11 pounds, 3 ounces at birth.

The Boss Shark

Boss is credited with customizing and designing a shoe to help players with shin splints. Nike later made a shoe called the "Boss Shark."

"It was one of the first football shoes to have a midsole, like a jogging shoe," Boss said. "Before then, all football shoes were basically flat. Now most football shoes have some means of shock absorption."

Greg Lafleur

Greg Lafleur came to LSU in 1976 from the tiny town of Ville Platte in central Louisiana, a skinny quarterback in high school who was signed as a wide receiver. He was 6'4", 180 pounds.

In 1977, Lafleur and his roommate were competing for the wide receiver spot. His roommate? Future NFL star Carlos Carson. "We were going to alternate every other play," Lafleur recalled. "The second game of the season we played Rice, and we get the ball on the 20. Carlos went into the game first. They throw an 80-yard touchdown pass to Carlos. I'm like, 'Damn, I've got to have a big play.'

"The next time we get the ball, I went in and we ran a running play. The next play, Carlos goes into the game and they throw a 65-yard pass for a touchdown. And the next time he goes in he catches a 35-yard pass for a touchdown. So I didn't get to play after that.

"He catches a fourth consecutive touchdown pass. And then he catches a fifth consecutive touchdown pass. And

Greg Lafleur. Courtesy of LSU Sports Information.

the next game we play at Florida, he catches another touchdown pass."

Details not withstanding–Carson's TD catches against Rice were for 22, 29, 63, 20 and 67 yards–Lafluer was in trouble.

"He and I were competing for the same spot, and so I never played another down after that. I was a sophomore that year and played a game and a half. Then my junior year they moved me to tight end, and then they signed the best tight end in the country, Malcolm Scott. He went on and played for the Giants for a few years.

"My senior year, they changed coaching staffs. Jerry Stovall came in and they played two tight ends, and Malcolm and I both played my senior year."

Lafleur, now athletic director at Southwest Texas, caught 18 passes that season, none for touchdowns, but was still drafted in the third round by the Philadelphia Eagles. At the end of training camp he was cut and picked up by the St. Louis Cardinals, where he had a six-year career. He played for the Indianapolis Colts before getting into athletic administration at LSU.

"My career was kind of different," Lafleur said with a smile.

Trainer Rivalry

The head trainers for LSU, Tommy Moffett, and Tennessee, Johnny Long, are both protégés of Baton Rouge strength coach guru Gayle Hatch. Accordingly, the LSU-Tennessee game has its own prize for the winners: The Gayle Hatch Cup, which has been contested three times. The winning trainer keeps it until the next matchup. LSU beat Tennessee in Tiger Stadium in overtime in 2000, 38-31. Then Tennessee beat the Tigers in Knoxville 26-18 in the 2001 regular season. LSU got it back in December 2001 when the Tigers stunned the Vols in the SEC championship game, 31-20.

And the Hero Was ...

Speaking of that, when LSU beat Tennessee in the SEC title tilt, reserve quarterback Matt Mauck was named the game's MVP. He entered the game when starter Rohan Davey was injured.

"You've got in the back of your mind that Tennessee has a really good front, and Ro, not that he was injury-prone, but he'd been hurt in the past, and we were playing on turf and that's never a good thing," Mauck said. "So I had it in the back of my mind that, hey, I might get a shot this week.

"I was thinking Ro was going to play the whole game and I was going to sit down and give signs and not do much at all and have a great seat for the game. But you also want to prepare yourself a little bit, which I do every week in practice, to know what you're doing, have the right calls, the right reads, things like that. But to tell you the truth I really didn't have an [inkling] that I was going to play."

When Davey got hurt, Mauck was totally relaxed.

"He got hit, but I didn't think anything of it. [I]turned to someone and was talking to them and heard, 'Mauck, get ready!' So I ran over, maybe threw one or two balls, and just went straight out there. Maybe it was better that I didn't have any time to think about it."

Mauck rushed for 43 yards and had two touchdowns, including the game-winner.

"It sounds a lot better than what it was, probably. I played a total of [one] game, basically, and that was it. I try not to think of it like I did anything spectacular. I did what I was supposed to do. That's your job. Backup quarterback, you're supposed to be able to come in and at least manage the game, and I thought I was successful at that."

Robert "Red" Ryder

Ryder, from Alexandria, played at LSU from 1966-69 and was captain of the 1969 team. The offensive lineman enjoyed recalling his "moment of fame," which came during the 1969 Auburn game in Tiger Stadium. After the game, he got the game ball.

That was the contest that included LSU scoring a touchdown on a halfback option pass from Jimmy Gilbert to Andy Hamilton on the first play of the game. Later, the Tigers gave back a field goal to score the winning TD in a 21-20 victory.

"We literally practiced [the option pass] all week long," Ryder recalled. "The key to the play, because it was run to the split-end side, was [whether I] could pull and stop the defensive end on the split-end side and keep him from disrupting the play.

"We run the play and sure enough, I dive and disrupt the guy long enough for us to get the play off. I made that block and made it work and that was the reason I thought Coach Mac gave me the game ball."

Later in the game, LSU was setting up for a field goal, and Ryder got beat by a defensive lineman. The kick by Mark Lumpkin was good, but Lumpkin got roughed up by Ryder's man. McClendon chose to take the points off the board and take the penalty. LSU scored what turned out to be the winning TD, and George Bevan blocked what would have been Auburn's game-tying, point-after-touchdown try.

After the game, Alexandria's Bill Carter, Ryder's hometown sports writer, started asking questions. Ryder groaned, "[He] heard that I got the game ball. He walks up to coach Mac and says, 'Coach, I understand you gave the game ball to Red Ryder.' And he said, 'Why'd you do that?' And Mac told him, 'Because if he hadn't missed the block we would have lost the football game!'"

Eat Where?

L SU strength coach Tommy Moffett swears by this story from September 11, 2001, about Bryce Wyatt, a defensive lineman from Lake Charles, Louisiana.

"When news got out that the planes had flown into the World Trade Center and the Pentagon had been hit by [another] airplane, Bryce said 'Where are we gonna eat?' And we asked him, 'What are you talking about?' And he said, 'The Pentagon.'

"The Pentagon [dining hall at LSU] is where we eat. Bryce had no idea."

A Tommy Casanova Memory

M ike Demarie was an offensive guard from Lake Charles. Future All-American Tommy Casanova (LSU 1969-71), whom many regard as the greatest all-around athlete to ever play for LSU, recalled a game against Auburn. It was a day game on national TV in Tiger Stadium, which LSU won 21-20.

"Mike was an offensive guard from LaGrange. We were freshmen together. Mike weighed about 230 and was about 5'9". Solid. Everybody he played outweighed him by 40 or 50 pounds. But he was so strong and so quick; he'd get up under 'em and just root 'em out.

"We were playing Auburn. We were both ranked; they were like No. 4 and we were like No. 6."

Casanova recalled that Demarie was "just tearing this guy up and finally this guy just rears back and head [butts] him on the side of the head. I mean it sent him to another world. He was on the sideline and didn't know where he was."

Demarie got sent to the locker room with the trainers. Casanova laughed.

"They took him to the showers, which were on one side. They take all of his clothes off and clean him up and put a towel around his waist, and they're walking him down to the training room where he passes the chute [out to the field] and when he does he hears the crowd roar.

"He thinks: 'Game time, I need to be there.' And he bolts for the door. And we come in at halftime and there's this writhing mass of white. Back in the day we had all these student trainers in their white outfits, and they tackle him about halfway to the door. And he's shedding them like water off a duck's back and there's this writhing mass of white uniforms and this huge body trying to get out.

"They just kept piling on him, and we came walking in wondering what it was. But he came that close to running through those goal posts buck naked on national television."

Casanova said he told Demarie recently, "That will be the last thing I remember before they bury me. That's something you never, ever forget."

Nice View

L SU was loaded at running back when Kevin Faulk played for the Tigers from 1995-98. One time, his replacement, Rondell Mealey, was having a heck of game. Running backs coach Mike Haywood said he turned to Faulk.

"I asked him, 'Are you ready to go back in?' He said, 'No, I'm enjoying the show too much.'"

Boots Garland

Garland is best known for his work as a speed coach but is not afraid to tell an "Oral" joke.

"I started in school here in 1951, so you can imagine how many standouts I saw come through," Garland said. "Of course, I went for four terms, Truman, Eisenhower, Kennedy, Johnson, whatever.

"At any rate, when Coach McClendon was here, God bless him, he got a bunch of kids hurt. And the reporter asked him how he was going to get them well. And Coach Mac, he said, 'How can I get all these people well? Who do you think I am, Orville Roberts?'"

More Boots

"In the spring of 1972 I was assisting in track and a quarterback came out and said 'I need to get faster and quicker.' I said, 'No kidding, Dick Tracy.' He said he needed to get his 100 down, so we did about seven weeks' worth of work and he did pretty well after that. And his name was Bert Jones. I saw him recently. Bert is the product of an uncluttered mind. He had me come up to Ruston once to work with his younger brother Tom. And he told me, 'Coach, Tom is going to be a big boy. He hasn't even grown into his teeth yet.'

"Excuse me?"

Rumble in the Bayou

Verge Ausberry (LSU 1986-89) is now an assistant athletic director at LSU.

The linebacker from New Iberia, La., said his most memorable game as an LSU player was the "Earthquake Game," when LSU defeated Auburn 7-6 in 1988. The resulting roar from Tiger Stadium actually registered on a seismograph on the LSU campus.

A Favorite Moment?

Ausberry recalled attending a speaking engagement with head coach Bill Arnsparger.

"One of the guys asked a question about whether we were going to use a 3-4 or a 4-3 defense.

"And he said, 'That's not a defense, sir.' And the guy said sure they were, a 3-4 or a 4-3.

"And Coach Arnsparger told him, 'It takes 11 people to play defense.' And the crowd just roared."

Pro Football Hall of Famers

There are three former Tigers enshrined in the Pro Football Hall of Fame in Canton, Ohio: Steve Van Buren, Y. A. Tittle and Jimmy Taylor.

Steve Van Buren

Van Buren, drafted in the first round (fifth overall) by the Philadelphia Eagles in 1944, was born in British Honduras. His career at LSU (1941-43) was well capped by his senior year, when he made the All-SEC team and had a big performance in the 1944 Orange Bowl. LSU beat Texas A&M 19-14 as Van Buren ran for one touchdown and passed for another in the second quarter and then ran for a 63-yard TD in the third quarter. It was his 16th TD of the season, an LSU record until Charles Alexander scored 17 in 1977.

Steve Van Buren exhibit in the Pro Football Hall of Fame. Courtesy of Lee Feinswog.

"I had come to LSU out of Warren Easton High School in New Orleans," Van Buren told the Pro Football Hall of Fame. "My scholarship was at an end. [Coach Bernie] Moore put me in the backfield and I blocked for Al Dark.

"Dark was a pretty good football player and would probably have made it in the pros, although he had the skinniest legs you ever saw."

Dark, of course, went on to a big-time major-league baseball career.

Van Buren, obviously not a big talker, said the following upon his induction to the Hall of Fame in 1965:

"Thank you, Clarke Hinkle [the Hall of Famer who introduced him]. I'm certainly glad to have broken your record. Since you people can't hear too good and I'm not too good a speaker, I won't say much, but it's certainly an honor to be here. The two days I've spent in Canton will certainly bring me back every year from now on. Thank you very much."

Y. A. Tittle

The Y. A. stands for Yelberton Abraham. He came to LSU from Marshall, Texas, and played from 1944-47, making All-SEC the last two years.

Tittle went on to star with the Baltimore Colts, the San Francisco 49ers and then the New York Giants, where he was the NFL MVP in 1961 and '63.

"At LSU, I was a 55-minute man. I liked to

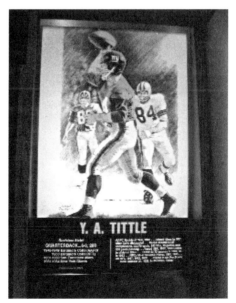

Y. A. Tittle exhibit in the Pro Football Hall of Fame. Courtesy of Lee Feinswog.

tackle–I'm no piece of china," Tittle said as a pro. He was drafted sixth overall by the Detroit Lions in the 1948 draft.

At his induction in 1971, he went on quite a bit longer than Van Buren. Tittle thanked his college coach, Bernie Moore, "who convinced me that I was good enough to be a pro."

Jimmy Taylor

Jimmy Taylor exhibit in the Pro Football Hall of Fame. Courtesy of Lee Feinswog.

For many LSU fans, no Tiger is held in higher regard than Baton Rouge's Jimmy Taylor (LSU 1956-67), a 1957 All-American who was named MVP of the 1958 Senior Bowl. He was a fantastic pro player, a fullback who personified the "run to daylight" mentality of the champion Green Bay Packers in the early to mid-1960s. He finished his career with the New Orleans Saints.

When he was inducted in 1976, Taylor didn't forget his roots. He said, "Charles McClendon and Paul Dietzel were coaches at LSU who certainly had the confidence to stay with me and give me the opportunity to play college football."

Cannon's Ring

The first AFL championship ring is on display in the Pro Football Hall of Fame. Along with it is a plaque that reads:

"On Jan. 1, 1961, the Houston Oilers won the first AFL championship by defeating the L.A. Chargers 24-16. In commemoration of that event, Oilers president K. S. (Bud) Adams Jr. in 1979 presented rings to all members of the 1960 Oilers. The ring on display was made for Billy Cannon, who, as a Louisiana State All-American, became the first big college star to sign with the new AFL."

College Football Hall of Fame

LSU is incredibly well represented at the College Football Hall in South Bend, Ind.

Coaches

Even the most diehard of Tiger fans might be surprised to know that Dana X. Bible, enshrined in 1951, is listed as a former LSU coach. Bible's resume includes coaching stops at Mississippi College, Texas A&M, Texas, LSU and Nebraska. Bible is listed as one of three head coaches of the 1916 Tigers, taking over and going 1-0-2. He was enshrined in 1951, having had the bulk of his success at Nebraska and Texas.

Michael Donahue coached at LSU from 1923-27, compiling a record of 23-19-3. The Yale graduate, enshrined in 1951, also coached at Auburn.

The winningest coach in LSU history, Charles McClendon, was inducted in 1986. His coaching career at LSU, from 1962-79, saw him compile a record of 137-59-7.

And Bernie Moore, LSU's coach from 1935-47, was inducted in 1954. Moore, like Bible, was a graduate of Carson-Newman College. He went 83-39-6 in 13 years, then the longest tenure of any LSU coach. He resigned in 1947 to become commissioner of the Southeastern Conference.

Players

Another LSU coach in the College Hall, Gaynell Tinsley (LSU 1934-36), was enshrined for his efforts as a player. Tinsley was inducted in 1956 after a great career as a receiver in the mid-1930s. Tinsley was quarterback Abe Mickal's favorite target, and he also played baseball. The product of Hainesville, Louisiana, was team captain in both sports and later played pro football for the Chicago Bears before returning to LSU as a coach. As head coach from 1948-54, he compiled a record of 35-34-6.

Ken Kavanaugh (LSU 1937-39) of Little Rock, Ark., was inducted in 1963. The end, a favorite target of Leo Bird's, was credited with being part of an aerial combination unrivaled in the South in the 1930s. Passing wasn't the primary form of attack in those days, yet Kavanaugh caught 30 passes in 1939 to lead the nation's receivers and earn MVP honors in the SEC. He later became an All-Pro for the Chicago Bears. During World War II he served as a bomber pilot and flew 30 missions over Germany, winning the Distinguished Flying Cross and the Air Medal with four Oak Clusters.

Abe Mickal (LSU 1933-35) was a halfback inducted in 1967. He was called "Miracle" Abe Mickal for his pinpoint passing in an era when the ball was bigger and rounder than it is today. The product of McComb, Miss., threw a 65-yard TD pass to Gaynell Tinsley to beat Southern Methodist that was a record for longest scoring pass in the South. LSU was 23-4-5 in his career.

Doc Fenton (LSU 1907-09) came to LSU from Pennsylvania, where he played at Mansfield State before transferring to LSU. He played end and place-kicker and was part of LSU's team that became the first American team to play a football game in a foreign country as the Tigers beat Havana University in Cuba, 56-0. Fenton later became LSU's quarterback.

Tommy Casanova (LSU 1969-71) was a two-time All-American defensive back who also played offense and returned punts and kicks. He had a standout career in the NFL with the Cincinnati Bengals. Casanova, from Crowley, La., is an ophthalmologist in his hometown and a state senator.

And Then Some

If you go to the College Football Hall of Fame, you'll see LSU in many places on the time line that traces the game through the years. A kiosk featuring great moments in college football includes Billy Cannon's 89-yard punt return to beat Ole Miss in 1959. LSU's many bowl game appearances are noted, Cannon's Heisman portrait is on exhibit, and LSU's national championship team of 1958 is recognized.

CHAPTER 11

Charles
McClendon

Though Nick Saban might finally be its answer, LSU has essentially been trying to replace Charles McClendon since 1979.

After he was forced out, Bo Rein got the job but died in a plane crash. Jerry Stovall, Bill Arnsparger, Mike Archer, Curley Hallman, Gerry DiNardo and Hal Hunter came and went. Much like Alabama, where they're still trying to replace Bear Bryant, LSU has never found anyone to fill McClendon's shoes.

"That makes me feel mighty good. I hadn't thought about it in those terms," McClendon said in November 2000. "But I've had a great feeling for LSU even though I haven't been there. In fact, when I was living in Florida, the Florida-LSU game was always the turning point. We'd watch it and then come back here for the rest of the winter."

McClendon had a .692 winning percentage and took LSU to 13 bowls in 18 years.

Coach Mac died of cancer in December 2001. I had the good fortune to interview him late in 2000 when he spent an hour on *Sports Monday*, a live TV show in Baton Rouge. Callers who got through were genuinely thrilled to talk to the coach who contributed so many great moments to LSU football history.

Charles McClendon. Courtesy of LSU Sports Information.

Pressures of the Job

McClendon was head coach at LSU from 1962-79 and brought a style all his own.

"Coach Mac," lineman Tyler Lafauci recalled, "had a saying, 'Fellas, inside the five-yard line, you ought to be able to tell them what you're going to run and make it.'"

Most times they did. Perhaps it was because McClendon seemed to enjoy practice more than games.

"As coaches, we have more fun looking at tape in the spring than in the fall," Mac said. "In the fall you have things you have to do. In the spring you really see some of the things that went past you. So in the spring you get to see all the good things the fellas accomplished."

A Product of the Bear

McClendon played for coach Bear Bryant at Kentucky, in addition to being an assistant coach under him.

"I thought he was pretty mean, myself," McClendon said with a laugh. "That's what my players say, 'Coach, you made life so tough.' I can't believe that. They're good people and we can laugh about it now, so something good must have come from it.

"Anyway, the last time I coached against him was in Tiger Stadium, and Alabama was on our side of the field. I saw the fullback take a step back, so that meant they had to make room for the guard to pull for a fullback trap. I hollered out there, 'Fullback trap! Fullback trap!'

"Well, we stuffed them for a two-yard loss. The Alabama players went to the sidelines and told Coach Bryant that Coach Mac knows the automatics. I didn't know the automatic system. I just lucked up.

"But Coach Bryant wasn't going to take any chances. Any time they were on our side of the field on the near hash mark, they ran the play in the other direction.

"I had to laugh about it."

Beating the Bear

McClendon was the first of Bryant's former pupils to beat him.

"Beat him twice, which is one more than anyone else. But that's why I got relieved of my job, because they said I couldn't beat Coach Bryant. But you can't find anybody else who did either, with any consistency."

LSU's victory in 1969 was the last one over Alabama in Tiger Stadium until 2001.

"We were a better team, but they almost pulled it out in the fourth quarter. When we went out to the middle of the field after the game, I know our fans were wondering what we were talking about.

"I put my arm around him and said, dead serious, 'Coach, if you'd have won tonight I'd have gotten a gun and shot you.' And he just died laughing, because he knew how tense I was about that game."

According to Mac, Coach Bryant wasn't thrilled about the tradition of Saturday Night in Tiger Stadium.

"Coach Bryant at Alabama never wanted to play us on Saturday night. So he did everything he could with the networks to get us to play in the daytime. He didn't like nighttime football in Tiger Stadium."

Decline in the 1970s

In 1973 LSU was 9-0. The team lost to Alabama 21-7 and then lost to Tulane before going to the Orange Bowl and losing to Penn State and Joe Paterno.

"That was a big mistake, too. That Penn State team was loaded. I think they had 11 players who signed professional contracts the next year," McClendon said.

In 1974, LSU dipped to 5-5-1, followed by a 5-6 campaign in 1976. McClendon's teams rallied as the Tigers went a combined 30-16-1 in his final four seasons, including a victory in the 1979 Tangerine Bowl over Wake Forest.

McClendon blamed a couple of tough recruiting years.

"There's a fine line between winning and losing," he said.

He didn't blame politics.

"I was completely innocent if there were politics when I was coaching. I went the other way and did things so independently that if I went down, I would go down my way."

The Big Bucks

Much of the income for today's big-time college football coaches comes from their media work, which usually includes involvement in weekly television and radio shows. Two hours of this work can net a coach half a million dollars.

Charlie Mac was not so lucky.

After coaching a game in Tiger Stadium on Saturday night, Mac would go home, get a few hours' sleep, and then catch a small plane the next morning to Shreveport to tape his TV show.

"Did it for three years," McClendon said. "And my wife used to say, 'We won the game; can't you smile?' And I'd say, 'Honey, have you ever seen a dead man smile?'

"I was so tired. I could prick myself with a pin and not feel it, I was so tired. I didn't catch up with myself till about Wednesday. It was a tough, tough routine."

What's worse, often the travel was anything but smooth.

"I remember in a downpour trying to lie down in the plane, and I'd come completely out of my seat, it was such bad weather."

On top of his other responsibilities, McClendon spoke at the New Orleans Quarterback Club every Monday morning. And his salary? $18,000 per year.

Cholly Mac on the Media:

"I appreciated the media," McClendon said. "A lot of football coaches were afraid of the media. I wasn't. I wasn't smart enough to be afraid. They were my friends and they had a job to do, and I understood that job. I told them, 'Fellas, I may need a favor from you now and then, but it's up to your journalistic background as to whether you can help or not.' They put me on the spot sometimes, but I got along with the media."

Cholly Mac on Recruiting:

"One of the cute things about recruiting is that you go and visit with a recruit and the mother and father, and the mother would say, 'Coach, you'd better talk to John.' For courtesy reasons I would talk to her husband for about five minutes, but then I'd go right back to momma, because she's going to make that decision!"

A Nice Ring to It

Coach Mac wore a ring given to him by his teams that won the 1965 Sugar Bowl (over Syracuse) and the 1966 Cotton Bowl (over Arkansas).

"My players designed this and gave it to me. I am so proud of that '66 Cotton Bowl team because they're responsible for getting reunions together. That's what winning does for you. They'll always be close," said McClendon.

"We weren't supposed to win that Cotton Bowl. I had a crippled football team, with three quarterbacks injured, and it took all three of them for us to win. It was just a real blessing.

"[Arkansas] Coach [Frank] Broyles and I are good friends. After the game, he said, 'You kept us out of being national champs.' Oh, did we? I knew what the stakes were," McClendon said with a laugh.

"They had won 22 straight games and we put No. 23 jerseys on our players for two straight weeks because we were supposed to be victim No. 23. But we were not to be denied."

Teamwork

"We had the training, but we couldn't get bigger. We just weren't a big group of people," McClendon said of his teams. "We had to depend on speed and quickness. Opponents would compliment us and tell us that 11 people were always going after them, and that's what we were trying to accomplish."

Always Helping Out

Before his death, Coach Mac created The Charles McClendon Scholarship Foundation to benefit the children of former LSU football players. To contribute, mail checks to 5930 Menlo Drive, Baton Rouge, Louisiana 70808.

Gone, But Not Forgotten

When Coach McClendon died, the author went to his funeral, visited with many of his friends and former players and wrote the following memorium. It appeared December 18, 2001, in *The News-Star* (Monroe, La.) and in *Purple and Gold*, a magazine devoted to LSU athletics.

BATON ROUGE - They stood waiting, the line as long as 50 deep to get into the University Baptist Church last Monday morning.

It was for a funeral, but when they talked about Charles McClendon, his friends and admirers couldn't help but smile and laugh as they recalled the late LSU football coach.

"Coach Mac was really one of the great people in my life," former LSU and NFL great Tommy Casanova said. "Unfortunately I didn't realize it until we got away from football. But just to see the character and class that he had."

McClendon, the winningest football coach in LSU history, died Dec. 6 after a long battle with cancer. But right up to the end, he remained the upbeat, good-humored person his players and friends loved.

Many remarked about how he never lost his sense of humor. Or, more importantly, their sense of humor about him, because Mac could make you laugh. The late Paul Manasseh was the LSU sports information director for many of the Mac years. His son, Jimmy, smiled at the memories.

"My dad had McClendonisms," Manasseh said. "Like he called Charles Alexander 'Charles McAlexander.' Going to Georgia was 'Behind the bushes.' And his favorite one was 'It always ceases to amaze me.' That was his favorite one."

Or longtime friend Bill Bankhead, who recalled seeing Coach Mac for the first time after he lost his eye and Mac telling him not to feel sorry for him, because "I play a lot better golf with one eye than I did before."

McClendon was forced to resign, many say unfairly. All he did from 1962 to 1979 was go 137-59-7–that included just one losing season. Truth is, LSU's been trying to replace him ever since. Bill Arnsparger had a good run in the 1980s, and it appears Nick Saban is on the right track, but the LSU record is filled with coaches having good records in their first two seasons.

"He wasn't treated correctly [by LSU] but he never let it show," Casanova said. "He just handled it with dignity and class."

No, he always referred to his players as "my boys" and made it his job to create the Charles McClendon Scholarship Foundation, which was dedicated to children of former LSU players. He believed in the cause and worked hard at it.

"Coach Mac gave everything he had, just like with his foundation," said Nelson Stokley, the former LSU quarterback and Southwestern Louisiana football coach who also served as one of McClendon's assistants. "He was worried about others more than himself. I knew we all grew up because we had Coach Mac as a coach."

McClendon actually wrote his own message for the service last week. It included: "I want my family, players and friends to only share tears of happiness today. Let's all remember the good times while we were together ... I would like to be remembered as a family man, father, grandfather who loved his family, friends, profession and life in general. I have prayed that what little I could contribute to our society would help make the place we live a little better."

Few doubted that he had.

"The last several months of his life, the hardship that man went through, was not only difficult, but painful. And he never let it show," Casanova said. "You'd call him, you'd go visit him and he was always as cheerful as he could be and making the best out of a bad situation. I just think he was a great example for us, not just on the field but the way he lived his life. The world needs a whole lot more people like that."

The late Carl Maddox was a football coach for LSU and later its athletic director. His son, Mike, recalled meeting McClendon as a third-grader.

"He was the most affable guy," Maddox said. "It was like we had known each other for years. That made the greatest impression on me."

"The man knew so much more about the game and about life and about people than many folks gave him credit for," said Dick Walcott, a former area sports television reporter. "He really had an insight into the game.

"It was really a thrill being associated with Coach Mac over the years."

Attorney Mike Pharis was stumped.

"I don't have anything left to say. Everybody's said it all. He was a great man."

Paul Dietzel, 77, hired McClendon in the 1950s to help coach a team that eventually won the 1958 national championship. He revelled in telling stories of his lifelong friend, coincidentally realizing now that he's the only one still living from that LSU staff.

"Mac was a tough fighter," Dietzel said. "He never, ever, ever gave up. I really pray that he's in a better place, because he suffered a lot. We lost a fine man, but he'll never be forgotten, I know that."

CHAPTER 12

Joe Dean: Hirings and Firings

Joe Dean was LSU's athletic director from 1987-2001, but he came to Baton Rouge long before that, when he was a freshman basketball player in 1948. It was a long way from his home in Indiana, where football was an afterthought.

"Football in the South has always been such a way of life, and it was here," Dean said.

Dean was always a big sports fan, so he enjoyed LSU football games as a student.

"I loved it," he said, "We only had a handful of sports then, and the athletes were very close. Some of the football players were among my best friends. We ate together; we

Joe Dean. Courtesy of LSU Sports Information.

practically lived next to each other. It was a different time. We went to the football games and they came to the basketball games. It was really kind of special."

Dean formed lifetime friendships with such players as Zollie Toth (LSU 1945-49) of Pocahontas, Va.; Jimmy Barton (LSU 1949-51) of Marshall, Texas; Lee Hedges (LSU 1949-51) of Shreveport, La.; and Charlie Pevey (LSU 1946-49) of Jackson, Miss.

"Charlie was a war veteran and older. But I was close to a lot of the guys on the team. The other guard on the LSU freshman basketball team, Billy West (LSU 1949-51) played football and then came back and played basketball his senior year. Billy Baggett (from Beaumont, Texas, LSU 1949-51) was a friend. And Charlie Cusimano was a friend of mine."

Of course, they remained friends and worked together closely, because Cusimano was long regarded as the most influential member of the LSU Board of Supervisors when it came to Tiger athletics.

Cusimano, from New Orleans, played football at LSU in 1945 and again in 1948 and '49.

"Charlie was a 190-pound guard who could run his butt off," Dean recalled. "He had great speed. He was a very bright guy, too.

"And it was a different time, then, too, from that point of view. You never heard much of guys not going to class. Most everybody got a degree or worked hard to get one. Most of the guys had successful lives."

Mike Archer's Tenure

Dean became athletic director in February 1987, about three months after Mike Archer replaced Bill Arnsparger as LSU's football coach. Archer was just 33 when he was hired.

Arnsparger, of course, left LSU to become athletic director at Florida and more or less hand-picked his successor, which some LSU fans thought was a cruel joke. The hiring also came at an odd time, since the late Bob Brodhead had resigned as AD and Arnsparger made his power move with an interim, Larry Jones, running the show.

Archer started fast–LSU went 10-1-1 in his first season, capped by a stunning 30-13 victory over South Carolina in the 1987 Gator Bowl–but saw a steady decline after that. The Tigers were 8-4 in 1988, which included a 23-10 defeat in the Hall of Fame Bowl to Syracuse. That game marked the beginning of the end for LSU football for the next seasons.

Mike Archer. Courtesy of LSU Sports Information.

LSU finished 4-7 in 1989 and 5-6 in 1990, which was followed by four consecutive losing seasons during Curley Hallman's subsequent tenure.

"Mike was a very nice person, and I liked him, but he was very immature at that point," Dean said. "And very inexperienced. He had never even been a head high school coach. Looking back, I'm surprised that they hired him. But he was a very nice guy with above-average intelligence."

Some said he was a poor recruiter.

"Bud Davis knew early, before I did, that we had the wrong coach," Dean said of the former LSU chancellor, who was once head coach at Colorado. "He was analyzing his recruiting and we weren't getting good players. His staff was shaky; he had some internal problems. There were some loyalty problems. I had two or three of his assistants come to me and say, 'You've got to make a change. This guy can't make it.' That's pretty tough. It was guys I respected and one of them even told him he was coming to me."

Archer's Firing

The departure of Mike Archer is one of the more bizarre stories in LSU history.

Dean and Davis hired a headhunting search firm to scout out a few potential replacements. Interestingly, Joe Dean does that type of work now. "We decided in the middle of the year to hire a search firm, very quietly, to help us see who was out there," Dean said. The firm, Raycom from Charlotte, included Richard Gianini, now AD at Southern Miss, and Bill Carr, later the AD at Houston.

"I gave them a list of about 15 names and they looked at them. No one knew what school it was. What happened was I had to make a payment. I went to TAF [Tiger Athletic Foundation] to get it and someone in there blabbed. It was embarrassing for me because I really liked Mike."

Dean was in Lake Charles when sportswriter Scooter Hobbs asked him if he had employed a search firm. "I told him it was true."

Dean came back to Baton Rouge that night to meet with Archer and sports information director Herb Vincent. Dean told Archer: "I won't lie to you. I like you. You can say I messed up and shouldn't have done this. You've got the job, but we felt like we needed to know where we were. This goes on, but it's handled better. I apologize."

Davis apologized, too, a few days later, and told Archer if he still wanted to be the coach at LSU, he could remain so for one more year.

"I had told the chancellor that was fine and I would go along with that. And Mike said, 'I don't think I want it.' True story."

Hallman's Hiring

"**I**t was amazing, really," Dean said. To this day, to many LSU faithful, the hiring of Hallman was nothing short of amazing.

Dean said Allen Copping, then president of the LSU system, asked about Hallman, whose team at Southern Miss had beaten Alabama, Auburn and Florida State.

"Everywhere I turned someone would say to me, 'This guy can't miss,'" Dean explained. "I called John David Crow [AD at Texas A&M, where Hallman had been a positions coach], and he said, 'Joe, the guy will work his ass off and he communicates with blacks as well as anybody you've ever seen.' Which was true."

Dean said the only negative Crow brought up was that Hallman was a loner, "a very lone wolf."

Dean shook his head.

"Everybody thought he was a diamond in the rough," Dean said.

"But I knew after a year that he wasn't very bright."

Hallman's Demise

When Hallman was hired, bumper stickers popped up that read: "Crazy 'Bout Curley." After the first year, Hallman kept his sense of humor as he saw that people had cut them up and rearranged them to read: "Curley 'Bout Crazy."

Hallman fired offensive coordinator George Haffner in December. Haffner was heard to respond, "Merry Christmas."

Nonetheless, defensive coordinator Phil Bennett, who would later try to become the LSU coach, went to Dean. "He told me, 'We're signing good players. He can recruit. If he'll get a good offensive coordinator in here we can make this thing work.'"

Curley Hallman. Courtesy of LSU Sports Information.

"Curley called me and told me he wanted to hire Lynn Amedee. They had been together at A&M. I told him I would really think about that. I wouldn't tell him who to hire, but to think about him and be sure it was a right fit. It was a critical hire. So he hired him, and for whatever reason, the chemistry wasn't there."

Hallman's era proved to be a blight on LSU football. He earned a record of 5-6 in 1991, his first year, and went to 2-9 in 1992. LSU improved to 5-6 in 1993 with a 3-1 finish, but that didn't carry over in 1994, when LSU went 4-7.

"I had to fire him," Dean said. "There was nothing I could do. But I'll never forget this: Gerry DiNardo's very first spring training practice he said to me, 'Are you aware there's some talent here?' Oh, yeah, I was aware. There was some talent there.

"He was so close. There's a fine line between winning and losing. There's a lot of guys out there who aren't very smart, but they surround themselves with a hell of a staff and they coach the team."

Hallman, who got divorced as his tenure ended, was credited with a great line: "I lost my job, my wife divorced me and my dog died all in the same year. I sure miss the dog."

Curley, Out for the Day

Hallman scheduled an interview for this book in early April 2002. The author, already in Bloomington, Ind., to interview Gerry DiNardo, was planning to fly from there to Starkville, Miss. However, Hallman, the defensive backs coach at Mississippi State, broke the appointment, explaining that he had to do his taxes that day with his accountant and then go to Jackson to buy furniture on a special deal. People who knew Hallman from his time in Baton Rouge weren't surprised.

Hiring Gerry DiNardo

The job was first offered to Mack Brown, then head coach at North Carolina and now head coach at Texas. Brown, also a former head coach at Tulane, was once an assistant at LSU. But Brown wanted more money than LSU was offering at the time.

Dean even interviewed Ron Zook, then an assistant at Florida. Zook, who eventually went to the New Orleans Saints, ultimately replaced Steve Spurrier at Florida.

"And I met Bill Snyder [head coach at Kansas State] at the Hyatt Hotel in downtown Kansas City and we spent an entire afternoon," Dean said. "He worked for a guy at Iowa who's retired now, Hayden Fry, and Hayden is a pretty good friend of mine. He and Charlie Cusimano [former LSU player and longtime member of the LSU Board of Supervisors] are close. They were in the Marine Corps together.

"Hayden called me and told me, 'Joe, this guy is really good and I think he may have a little interest in your job. But you've got to handle this really carefully.' I asked him to be the go-between and he said he would."

So they met in Kansas City, and Dean did everything but offer the job to Snyder.

"We had a great visit. He's a fine man. Obviously a damn good football coach. Not loaded with personality. What you see is what you get. He's a good manager. We could have probably hired him."

But Snyder called a couple of days later and told Dean K-State was where he needed to be. History shows Snyder made the right call, because his program has really flourished.

Then LSU turned its serious attention to Pat Sullivan, the former Heisman Trophy winner from Auburn who had just finished a winning season at Texas Christian University and was preparing for the Independence Bowl.

"When I interviewed Pat Sullivan I said, 'You have a buyout.' He said, 'Yes I do, but I can handle it.'

"I told Pat, 'I talked to your AD and he told me you had a very large buyout and somebody's going to have to pay it.' We had a big conversation about that. He told me he would handle it, but he was a nice, naïve kind of guy in a lot of ways."

At that point, the search was down to Sullivan and Vanderbilt coach Gerry DiNardo. Dean brought them both to Baton Rouge for interviews.

"DiNardo is the greatest interview of all time," Dean said. "He's entertaining, funny, smart, you're so attracted to him when you interview him. It's unbelievable as hell."

Sullivan's Demise

There were seven people at LSU president Allen Copping's house when a vote was taken, including Copping, Dean and Chancellor Bud Davis.

"I voted for DiNardo, but Sullivan got the job on a 4-3 vote. And Milton Womack [of the LSU Board of Supervisors] said, 'You seem pretty strong for Gerry DiNardo.' And I said, 'I am, I think his personality would be pretty engaging here. He's very smart and I think he'd be successful.' But I knew the alumni would buy Sullivan easier than they would Gerry DiNardo.

"Well, we get out in the garage, and Milton, who had voted for Pat Sullivan, said to me, 'Joe, it wouldn't take a lot for me to change my mind on this. If we end up with DiNardo it won't bother me.'

Anyway, that night I called Pat Sullivan and told him the job was his. He was very excited.

"It was Wednesday. Sullivan was offered a salary of $350,000," Dean said. Problem was, his buyout at TCU was more like $400,000. On Thursday, Sullivan called Dean to tell him his buyout was not something that would go away.

Dean remembered, "I told him, 'Pat, I have a real problem here. We had an agreement. My university is not going to send $400,000 to your university. The publicity would be very bad and it's just not something to do.' DiNardo told me, 'Yeah, I have a buyout. It's my responsibility and I'll handle it. Don't ever bring it up again.'"

DiNardo, in fact, did have a problem with his buyout, but settled it with Vanderbilt after he left LSU.

"Pat wanted me to help him figure out something, come up with a way," Dean continued. "Like all football coaches, they think, 'Well, you want me, work it out for me.' I'll bet you we talked eight times. And then he puts an agent on me out of Little Rock."

That Friday the LSU Board of Supervisors planned to meet in New Orleans.

"I needed a coach. At six in the morning, I called DiNardo and told him I might still work this out. I called Phil Bennett and asked him to have coffee."

Bennett, who was Hallman's defensive coordinator and was still on LSU's payroll, had interviewed for the LSU job himself, knowing he was a long shot.

"Phil told me, 'You will make a mistake hiring Pat Sullivan. He's a nice guy but he's not a good football coach. Everybody knows that. The other guy [DiNardo] is better. I'm going to tell you that right now.' He was very accurate. It gave me more confidence that what I thought was right."

Sold on DiNardo

On the way to New Orleans, with sports information director Herb Vincent behind the wheel, the Tiger Athletic Foundation's Richard Gill tried to talk Dean out of hiring DiNardo.

Nick Saban. Courtesy of Steve Franz/LSU Sports Information.

"I made a good speech to the board, kind of an emotional speech," Dean said. "And Allen Copping, God bless him, stood up and he said, 'I support Joe Dean. He's a good athletic director and he's our man.'

"I walked out of the meeting and called DiNardo."

DiNardo, of course, won three bowl games in his first three years at LSU from 1995-97. Three years later, by the way, Sullivan was done at TCU. He resigned in 1997 but finished the season, with the Horned Frogs going 1-10.

Hiring Nick Saban

Gerry DiNardo's tenure went south after two losing seasons, including a 3-8 finish in 1999 in which he didn't coach the last game. That turned out to be a 35-10 LSU victory over Arkansas in which Hal Hunter acted as the interim head coach.

"We bounced around for a week. A lot of people don't know this, but I hired Chuck Neinas [former commissioner of the Big Eight and director of the College Football Association], and Gil Brandt, both, to help me with the search," Dean said.

This search, just as when he hired DiNardo to replace Hallman, proved tough for Dean.

"We decided that if we didn't hire somebody who was a head coach, we were going to interview Phil Bennett [then at Kansas State as defensive coordinator], Mark Richt [an assistant at Florida State who later got the Georgia job] and Gary Kubiak [an assistant with the Denver Broncos]. That's where we were.

"We did all but offer the job to Butch Davis [head coach at Miami who would leave the next year for the Cleveland Browns]."

Davis called Dean a couple of days later and passed. "He made a comment to me, 'Tell me why your job's better than mine.' At that point, he knew he had a good team. He's in an easier league; this is a tough job."

The Saban Connection

Dean interviewed Bennett and also Glen Mason, head coach at Minnesota. He was setting up more interviews when the phone rang. It was Sean Tuohy, a product of Newman High School in New Orleans who played basketball at Ole Miss. He's a businessman in Memphis who still does basketball radio broadcasts.

"Sean owns Taco Bells, three with Jimmy Sexton," Dean said.

Sexton is also a sports agent. One of his clients at the time was Michigan State football coach Nick Saban.

Sexton called Tuohy, who called Dean.

"He said to me, 'Might you be interested in Nick Saban?' And I told him, 'Sean, we'd be interested in anybody, right now, to be honest with you, who's a head coach.'"

Sexton called Dean soon after.

"He was making $600,000 at the time. Jimmy Sexton called me, and I'll never forget this, but he said, 'Joe, this won't be all about money.' And I told him, 'Jimmy, it's always about money. It's always about money.'"

At that time, no one knew just how much so.

Meeting in Memphis

Dean, LSU chancellor Mark Emmert, Richard Gill, Charlie Weems and Stanley Jacobs (of the LSU Board of Supervisors) met Saban at Sexton's home in Memphis on a Saturday afternoon. They hadn't discussed the money.

"It was very good. We probably talked for four hours. Jimmy Sexton in that meeting asked me what my plans were. I told him I was getting ready to retire. This was early December. Everybody was sitting right there. I told him we could discuss that. Everybody asked a lot of questions. It was tough for Nick.

"But he basically got the job by default. Hell, we didn't have anybody. Think about it a minute. Some guy could have called us out of the blue, and that happens, but it's so difficult to hire somebody. The average fan has no clue how tough it is."

Becoming a Millionaire and Then Some

"We broke to eat and Jimmy Sexton pulled me aside and said, 'The key to this contract for this guy will be protection on the backside. I think we might be able to work this out.' In other words, no buyout from his end and totally big buyout from us."

Still, no dollar figures had been thrown around, especially not $1.2 million per year.

"I was thinking nine [hundred thousand] or a million," Dean said. "We were always ready to pay what the marketplace was. But we didn't have anybody to pay market value! I would have paid Mack Brown a boatload of money, but no one knew that because we never got to that. You've got to pay to get the right person, but we never had the right guy. You pay what you have to pay, but why give money away?"

Sunday night, Sexton called Dean.

"I'll never forget this: He said, 'We've got to start at a million-two.' Let me just say this to you right here right now: I could have hired him in a heartbeat for one million dollars. I could have hired him for 900 [thousand], 950 [thousand]. This was an opening number. He was an agent, what was he going to do?"

Sexton wanted to hear back that night. Dean said he called LSU chancellor Emmert and told him of Sexton's request. He said, 'Let's pay it.' I said, 'Mark, I can get him for less money. I'm not negotiating with the coach, I'm negotiating with the agent.' But Mark didn't want to lose him."

Dean said Emmert consulted LSU president Bill Jenkins, then called back to OK the deal.

"I called Jimmy Sexton and said, 'Jimmy, we just hired a coach for a million-two. Remember your statement that it isn't about the money? What did I say? It's all about the money.' We both started laughing.

"Let me say this: Jimmy Sexton knew he had a pigeon on his hand. He knew."

Final Thoughts

Compiling stories and writing this book was really fun, more so than I ever imagined. I'm not a graduate of LSU, but I have always understood the significance of the school's football program to its fans and its impact on our community. Now, because of this project, my appreciation for all that is LSU football has grown tremendously.

If you're an LSU fan, you know. For example, as Larry White, now an assistant athletic director at Alabama and former sports information director at LSU, told me: "There's nothing like a football game in Tiger Stadium when the band strikes up that music," he said. "Da-da-da-da...it just makes the hair on the back of your neck stand up."

Or what the late great Charles McClendon said about recruiting Louisiana athletes to play for LSU: "He might not have the best of ability, but when that young man knows that his momma and daddy and girlfriend can be there to see him play, he's going to give 100 percent."

Me? I couldn't have given 100 percent to this book if I hadn't had some great help from my recruits. Scott McKay,

editor and publisher of *Purple and Gold*, a magazine devoted totally to LSU athletics, was a huge help. So was Jared
Wright, a student worker in the LSU sports information
department. Chris Macaluso also contributed. The help I
got from two guys who should be in their respective halls of
fame was immeasurable: Joe Horrigan of the Pro Football
Hall of Fame and Shawn Robinson of the College Football
Hall of Fame. And thank goodness for Andrea Albright and
Marybeth Lima, who wrote the delightful chapter on Mike
the Tiger.

Of course, none of this would have been possible without the gracious insight and quotes given by the assorted
LSU players, coaches and support personnel who were interviewed for this book. I feel especially grateful to have
shared time with Coach Mac before he died, met Paul
Dietzel, and visited with so many other insightful and col-
orful characters who are part of the LSU lore.

On the home front, even though they contributed
nothing to this project, you can't write a book without men-
tioning your kids, so Stacey and Kirk, congratulations, you're
in your first book. And, of course, there's my wife, Brenda,
who continually prodded me along with that daunting question, "Don't you have a book to go finish?"

Truth is, I wouldn't have made it without her support.
She can't wait for the next book.

In the meantime, thanks for reading *Tales from the LSU
Sidelines*. I leave it up to former LSU athletic director Joe
Dean to summarize why you probably did:

"It's a way of life," Dean said about LSU football. "It's
a social event, it's a party, a parade. So many people go and
never even watch the games. We estimate there are 20,000
people who come for the party.

"It's amazing, really. It's a unique thing that goes on
here on this campus on Saturday nights. It really is."

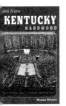